# Confessions
## of a Political
# Spouse

## James Schroeder

To
Mimi —
Old friends are
the best friends!
Jim
Schroeder

FULCRUM
GOLDEN, COLORADO

Library of Congress Cataloging-in-Publication Data
Schroeder, Jim.
  Confessions of a political spouse / by Jim Schroeder.
    p. cm.
  ISBN 978-1-55591-664-0 (pbk.)
  1. Schroeder, Jim. 2. Schroeder, Pat--Marriage. 3. Legislators' spouses--United States--Biography. 4. Husbands--United States--Biography. 5. Sex role--United States--Case studies. 6. Dual-career families--United States--Case studies. I. Title.
  E840.8.S36S37 2009
  328.73092--dc22
  [B]

                         2009007982

Printed in the United States of America by Bang Printing
0 9 8 7 6 5 4 3 2 1

Design: Jack Lenzo

Fulcrum Publishing
4690 Table Mountain Drive, Suite 100
Golden, Colorado 80403
800-992-2908 • 303-277-1623
www.fulcrumbooks.com

# Contents

# Introduction

*Nothing endows writers with a keener incentive to write, to plant their words where they will stay, than having something of their own to brandish.*
—Peter Davison

I once bought a book on writing. As I recall, the author's principal message and key advice was that if you want to write something—a story, a poem, an article, or even a book—you simply have to just do it: sit down and write. Her second piece of advice was pretty good, too: write about something you know.

Well, I cannot find that book (but I'll keep looking). It's buried somewhere on one of my many bookshelves. I love books. I have thousands of books, and I am usually reading two or three books at a time (when I'm not reading the latest issue of the *New York Review of Books*, *The New Yorker*, or *The Economist*). I can't throw a book away;

once read, they are old friends, having provided a source of past pleasure, learning, and enjoyment.

Almost every week I go into one of the big new mega-bookstores just to browse around, check on the latest best sellers, look through the sale tables, and have a cup of coffee. Unsurprisingly, I always end up buying something. Right now, like a lot of people, I've been reading books on Islam and the Middle East. Recently, I bought another copy of one of my favorite books, P. J. O'Rourke's *Holidays in Hell*, which I know I have two copies of somewhere (one autographed), but as usual, I can't find them!

Anyway, as I wandered through those thousands of books and examined the hundreds of new titles (including the hundreds of titles on the remainder or publishers' clearance tables), I wondered to myself with much trepidation and humility why anyone would want to buy a book by yours truly. What could I write about that someone would want to read or better still, fork over hard-earned dollars to buy? Well, dear reader, apparently you have made that decision, and I am eternally grateful. I hope that what you find in these pages—my confessions—will be interesting, entertaining, and thought-provoking; in other words, a good read.

So, what is this book about? What do I know about, that I think I can write about that may hold your interest and be worth your time and money? What something of my own can I "brandish"?

In August of 1962 I married a fellow Harvard Law School classmate, Patricia Nell Scott. Pat Schroeder is one of the most remarkable and successful women in America.

Pat represented Denver and served in Congress for twenty-four years. First elected in November 1972, she retired undefeated after twelve terms, in 1996. She explored running for the Democratic presidential nomination in 1987, and she was selected in the Gallup Poll in 1988 as one of the ten most respected women in America. After teaching at Princeton's Woodrow Wilson School of Public and International Affairs in the spring of 1997, she was appointed president and CEO of the Association of American Publishers, from which she retired in May 2009. She has served on several nonprofit corporate boards of directors and the Center for Human Rights of the American Bar Association. In December 1999, *The Denver Post* named Pat one of the ten most memorable Coloradans of the twentieth century.

As the title of this book suggests, it is a memoir of a political spouse. Though stories about Pat necessarily will be prominently featured—and there will be stories about politics and Congress, as these have been such important parts of both our lives—it is not a biography of Pat Schroeder. For that story, read the two books Pat has written, *Champion of the Great American Family* and *24 Years of House Work...and the Place Is Still a Mess*, or Joan A. Lowy's *Pat Schroeder: A Woman of the House*. Instead I will explore what it's like being "Mr. Pat Schroeder" and how I survived (and prospered and benefited) from this experience. For I—and Pat and I together—certainly had some interesting experiences throughout our careers.

I hope that my experiences and observations will transcend the personal and be of interest, and perhaps even of help, in particular to other "second-place" spouses (whether political or not), but also in general to dual-career couples. How should men deal with women, and especially successful women? Is a successful dual-career marriage possible? How do you handle it when your wife passes you by on the road to fame and fortune?

This is not a how-to book. I have no ten-point program for a successful dual-career marriage or seven steps for a political spouse. But I do hope I learned some valuable lessons and that they may be relevant, worthwhile, and of benefit to others. As you read on, I hope there will be a few laughs as well. If not, *Holidays in Hell* is still available at your local bookstore, and it's a classic!

—Jim Schroeder
Celebration, Florida
2009

# PART I

# Beginnings

*The ending is always right there in the beginning.*

— Professor Harry Stevenson, Morgan Freeman's
character in the 2007 film *Feast of Love*

CHAPTER 1

# Denver, Colorado, September 28, 1987

*The Democratic campaign will be duller if,*
*by September 1, Mrs. Schroeder concludes that the*
*dough is just not there. She stands out from the other*
*candidates for reasons other than the obvious one.*
—The Economist, August 27, 1987

They say—whoever "they" are—that all bad novels start out with that classic line "It was a dark and stormy night..." This is not a novel but a work of nonfiction, and I hope it will be a good one. So let me start out with something different: "It was a bright and sunny day..."

It was a bright and sunny day, one of those perfect fall days that Denverites love and have come to expect: a bright blue sky, warm temperatures, low humidity, and a light breeze along the Front Range, where dashes of gold aspen intermingled with dark green pines below snow-capped peaks.

Thousands of people, along with hundreds of reporters and media personnel from all over the country, were gathered around the Greek amphitheater in Denver's Civic Center Park, located between the Denver City and County

Building and the Colorado State Capitol. They had come to learn whether Denver's eight-term congresswoman and my wife, Pat Schroeder, would formally enter the race for the 1988 Democratic presidential nomination.

Other women had run for president, or at least had had their names placed in nomination. The first woman to run for president, as a candidate of the Equal Rights Party, was Victoria Woodhull, in 1872. She was followed by Belva Lockwood, also a candidate of the Equal Rights Party, in 1884. In later years, several other minor parties nominated women candidates. The first woman to have her name placed in nomination by a major political party was Senator Margaret Chase Smith, in 1964. Representative Shirley Chisholm and Representative Patsy Mink ran short, and largely symbolic, campaigns in 1972.

Would Pat's run for the nation's highest office be the first time a woman—and a mother at that—mounted an organized, serious presidential campaign for a major party's nomination?

Pat's exploratory efforts had started in June, almost by chance. As she had done in 1984, Pat began the year as one of Senator Gary Hart's national campaign codirectors. When Gary withdrew from the field in May, after the infamous Donna Rice escapade, many liberal Democrats, including a lot of women, began to look for another candidate. And why not a woman? Why not continue to build on the legacy of Geraldine Ferraro's selection as Walter Mondale's vice-presidential running mate in 1984?

I was working in my law firm's Bangkok office in early June of 1987 when my partner showed me a copy of *USA*

*Today.* "Well, I guess your wife has been busy while you were gone," he said. I picked up the paper and there was her picture and the headline "Pat Schroeder considering running for President." It's amazing, the trouble your wife can get into when you leave town for a few weeks!

When I returned to Washington, I found that Pat was serious; she wanted to explore the possibility of running, to test the waters, to see if there was the necessary political and financial support for her candidacy. Could she—could a woman—be a viable national candidate?

We formed an exploratory committee and set up operations in several vacant offices in my law firm's Washington building, on Seventeenth Street. I told my firm I would be taking a leave of absence for the rest of the summer. Our goal was to raise $2 million by September and see what kind of support we could develop. As Pat said, "No dough, no go." We needed sufficient funds to run something other than a symbolic campaign and prove Pat was a credible candidate.

I remember running into Congressman Bob Matsui in an elevator at the Rayburn House Office Building. When he asked me how things were going, I said we were trying to raise $2 million by September. He laughed and said, "I'm thinking about running for the Senate from California, and I'm trying to raise $6 million."

Pat's efforts were serious, and she was a potentially formidable candidate. In January 1987, the *LA Times* published a poll showing how Democratic presidential hopefuls rated among delegates to the California Democratic Convention. At that time, thirteen names were included. Pat was "regarded favorably" by 63 percent of those polled and was fourth overall; she followed New York governor Mario Cuomo, Gary Hart, and Jesse Jackson. By June, Governor Cuomo had decided not to run and Hart had dropped out.

During the summer, Pat's exploratory efforts generated extensive press coverage and many enthusiastic support-ers, especially among women. The press loved Pat—she was energetic, attractive, quick-witted, and talked common sense on tough issues. After seven years of Reagan's "me first" era of ever larger debt and federal government inaction and inefficiency, Pat called for "a rendezvous with reality." It became, for many in the media, a contest featuring Snow White (Pat) and the Seven Dwarfs: Senators Al Gore (D-TN), Joe Biden (D-DE), and Paul Simon (D-IL); Governors Mike Dukakis (D-MA) and Bruce Babbitt (D-AZ); Representative Dick Gebhardt (D-MO); and Jesse Jackson.

The respected Field (California) Poll sampled almost four hundred registered Democratic voters between July 24 and August 1 as to their preferences in this eight-candidate field. Governor Dukakis and Reverend Jackson were virtu-ally tied as the first pick, but Pat ran a surprising third.

Although Pat was not a declared candidate, I was invited to attend a spouses debate in Wisconsin. When I couldn't make it, Hattie Babbitt, Bruce's wife, announced that "Jim Schroeder was unable to attend because he couldn't decide what to wear." (Hattie and Bruce are good friends of ours, and Hattie and I always laugh about this "gender discrimination.")

Money was the problem. By September we had raised almost $1 million, a tidy sum to be sure, and all small grassroots contributions, but it was only half of our stated goal. "The mother's milk of politics" had flowed, but not enough. I later marveled at Governor Howard Dean's use of the Internet and wondered, "What if?" If we'd had such a tool in 1987, things might have gone differently.

As we were getting ready to fly back to Denver in September for Pat's announcement, I wrote her a personal memo in longhand urging her to do what she wanted to do and what she felt was right. I think that she knew, and I knew, that the realistic course was not to run. The practical and financial barriers were just too great.

Then, on Friday, I received three calls. First, Lou Harris, the pollster, called and advised that Pat was running third in his polling, trailing only Dukakis and Jackson. He said he thought her support was solid and she could maintain and improve that position if she stayed in the race. Second, the director of an independent oil and gas operators' group called from Dallas and reported that his members were ready to support Pat, a westerner who was both knowledgeable and supportive of their interests. Third, the former state Democratic Party chairman of New Hampshire called and said he was ready to head up Pat's campaign in that key primary state.

So I rewrote the conclusion to my memo: "Pat, it's still up to you, but I think you can do it, and should do it."

This was not, however, her 1972 congressional race, run in a limited district. We were, after all, looking at a presidential campaign, held throughout the entire United States. Pat's political judgment has always been one of her greatest assets, and this time, her head prevailed over her heart.

On that bright, sunny September Colorado morning, she announced she would not formally enter the 1988 presidential race.

As she spoke to the assembled crowd—her family, friends, supporters, many women accompanied by their daughters—Pat's voice broke and tears filled her eyes. She quickly recovered, but a picture of Pat with her head on my shoulder is the one that most newspapers ran the next day.

Pat was roundly criticized for crying, especially by some women reporters. Since Senator Ed Muskie had wept at a press conference in 1972 over published attacks against his wife, it had become an axiom of American politics that a politician could not cry in public. And now, a woman was doing it, seeming to confirm that women were too soft, not strong enough to be Commander in Chief and leader of the Free World. Pat's reply to that criticism: "Do you want someone with his—or her—finger on the nuclear red button who does not cry?"

In later years, Pat kept a file on the many male politicians who shed a few tears in public. It was a large file, and included President Reagan and Senator Bob Dole, among others. The numbers continue to grow, and now include President H. W. Bush and House Republican Minority Leader John Boehner. There still appears to be a double standard, however. A woman politician who cries in public does so at her peril. Hillary Clinton's teary response to a voter's question in New Hampshire drew a lot of criticism; on the flip side, it may have helped her primary campaign, because she showed a softer, more emotional side.

How would Pat have done if she had stayed in the

presidential race? *Newsweek* did a poll of likely voters that fall of 1987, comparing certain "positive qualities" of the average male Democratic candidates and Pat. Of the nine categories, she led in eight, often by ten to fifteen percentage points. For example, as "someone you would be proud to have as President," Pat's percentage deviation was a plus 15 percent; as "someone you can trust," it was a plus 11 percent; as someone who "cares about the average American," a plus 9 percent; and as a "strong and decisive leader," a plus 4 percent. Her only negative was "experience to be President," a minus 2 percent.

What kind of experience a person has had, and the value and importance of that experience, is often in the eye of the beholder. Witness Governor Sarah Palin. On the other hand, Senator Clinton based her presidential campaign, at least initially, on her experience. Remember the red telephone and the 3:00 AM phone call?

Although she once disavowed any resemblance to Tammy Wynette, Hillary did "stand by her man" during the Lewinsky affair. And Bill stood by Hillary throughout her 2008 presidential campaign, and would have been a terrific First Man if Hillary had become our first woman president. As for me, I love Tammy Wynette and was proud to stand by my woman. I was glad to be able to stand alongside Pat, and in the words of another song, give her a shoulder to cry on.

CHAPTER 2
# This Guy Schroeder
—Title of 1970 campaign brochure for
Colorado State House of Representatives

Science tells us that 50 percent of a child's development depends on the gene pool, and 50 percent on socioeconomic environmental factors. Imagine planting corn. Is the seed a good hybrid, disease resistant, planted in rich, black soil? Or is it a weak, deficient seed, scattered on rocky, sandy ground? Will the seed—and the young plant—receive adequate sun and water, or suffer from drought or flood? Will the young plant receive fertilizer and pesticides, or be engulfed by weeds and become the victim of worms, bugs, and locusts? Will the final product be a golden ear of healthy corn, or a disappointing stock of shrunken and inedible produce? Much depends on the farmer, his initial choices, and then on his subsequent care and skills. But he must also cope with and attempt to control—or even overcome—the outside forces of nature.

Heredity and environment. What we started with. What forces and experiences affect us. Chance and choice.

I was born on April 19, 1936, into an upper middle-class home in the affluent Chicago suburb of Elmhurst,

Illinois. My mother, Thelma, a schoolteacher and graduate of the University of Chicago, was a Bible Belt Christian raised on a farm outside Charleston, Illinois. Her father, Zaccheus Boone White, my grandfather, was a special person: tall, distinguished, an excellent farmer, and a devout Christian. He served as Sunday school superintendent of the Harrison Street Church of God for fifty years. The Church of God was a Protestant evangelical denomination founded in the 1800s, and it was strongly antislavery. Granddad Zach's father, Isaac, and his father, Silas, were both ordained ministers in the Church of God. Silas White married Mary J. Boone, a grandniece of the famous Kentuckian Daniel Boone, hence my Granddad Zach's middle name. My great-great grandfather on my grandmother's side, George Sandoe, was also a minister, and chaplain of the 123rd Illinois Volunteer Infantry Regiment in the Civil War. The Illinois 123rd was one of Grant's most dependable regiments and fought with distinction at Perryville, Kentucky, and Chattanooga and Chickamauga, Tennessee. I have framed a letter that he wrote my great-great grandmother Josephine when the 123rd was with Sherman outside Atlanta in July 1864.

My father, Paul, was a dentist, a graduate of the University of Louisville, and the only one of five children to attend college. He worked his way through dental school by playing the violin in an orchestra that worked on riverboats cruising the Ohio. My German grandfather, Fredrick Wilhelm Schroeder, came from Semlow, Pomerania, in northeastern Germany. After immigrating to the United States in the 1880s and marrying my German grandmother,

Minnie, my grandfather Schroeder, a tailor, established a men's clothing store in Woodstock, Illinois.

I never knew my paternal grandfather, as he died before my parents were married. I think, however, that he passed along some pretty good German genes: order, discipline, hard work, religious belief, family values, patriotism. Three of his sons, including my father, served in the US Army in World War I. His oldest son, Emil—the only other child to marry—had a son, Bob, who served in the US Navy in World War II and Korea, and two daughters, Bea and Ruth, who were nurses during World War II. After the war, my cousin, Dr. Ruth, became one of the first women to graduate from Harvard Medical School.

I never knew my grandmother White, who also passed away before my parents were married. She was, according to all reports, a remarkable woman, the "Martha Stewart" of Charleston, who catered local dinner parties for Eastern Illinois State Teachers College professors and their guests, earning extra money to help put my mother through college.

My mother, a devout Christian and daughter of downstate Illinois soil, was the primary force in my development. I was raised with love, with a sense of humility and grace toward life, and with tolerance and respect for others. Through my mother's teaching, whatever I did, I did my best, worked hard, didn't quit, and persevered. For example, several times I almost gave up on Scouting, but she wouldn't let me; I became an Eagle Scout because of her constant encouragement and support.

I did give up on the piano my sophomore year in high

school so I could play football. My mother said that someday I'd be sorry, but my father said he understood. He
loved sports, and I still am a loyal fan of the Chicago Cubs,
Bears, and Blackhawks. But I am sorry!

My father also instilled in me the value of hard work,
the importance of financial responsibility (he never had a
credit card), and the importance of politics. Both my parents
contributed to my love of music. One of my fondest memories of growing up was gathering around the phonograph on
a Sunday afternoon to listen to an opera or symphony, on a
RCA Victor 78 rpm record, no less—scratchy, but beautiful.

———

If you'd asked me about women when I was a young kid
growing up—and, of course, nobody did—I guess I would
have said they were equal to men—fellow human beings,
creatures of God—but different. They were special, and
merited consideration, courtesy, care—and sometimes,
protection. I kept that in mind one day when my baby
sister, Sandra, was playing in a sandbox and an older boy
threw sand at her. When she started crying, I picked up a
stone and threw it at him. My mother was not pleased, and
I was told that this was not the right way to help her—but
Sandy did stop crying.

As the good book says, God created man in his own
image, declared it good, and then rested. My wife says that
God then thought He could do better, so He created woman, and rested. We guys then add that thereafter, neither
man nor God has ever rested.

But let's move forward to environment and experience.

We all know that girls develop and mature earlier than boys—physically, mentally, socially. At a certain age, they begin to resemble Carrie Fisher with a bunch of Ewoks in *Star Wars*. I think I was like most guys in my day, and I suppose it's still true today: we didn't pay much attention to girls as different and special creatures until high school. We were too busy with other, more important pursuits, like sports.

High school was the great awakening and learning experience. First, I learned that girls were as smart as, and probably smarter than, boys. I graduated thirteenth in a class of approximately three hundred and fifty. The twelve who ranked ahead of me were all girls. That they were more conscientious and hard working than I probably helped their class standing. I wasn't surprised in later life, then, when strong and talented women began to assume a greater role in our nation's economic, social, and political development—and, of course, in my own life too.

Despite the strictures of the early 1950s, there was already the suspicion that women could succeed in almost any field that would open to them, including athletics. I marveled at the athletic ability of our cheerleaders and always picked Alice Aitken for my touch football team, starting back in sixth grade at Washington Elementary. Alice was almost six feet tall, well coordinated, and fast afoot. She was a good blocker and a terrific wide receiver. And, like many of today's women soccer and tennis stars, Alice was very attractive. In college she was elected homecoming queen at Auburn University.

I never had much luck with York High School girl-friends. For whatever reason, I found myself attracted to out-of-town girls, and usually older ones, at that. My most serious relationship was with Victoria Kneevers, from Sheboygan, Wisconsin, whom I had met on my American Field Service (AFS) summer in Germany. During my senior year at York, Torri was already a freshman at Carlton College in Minnesota. We did, however, manage to stay in touch, and Torri was my date for our graduation prom and parties.

Those were the days, when girls were mysterious and innocent and guys "explored" with a sense of excitement but also fear: fear of commitment, of breaking the rules, of pregnancy. I never "scored a homerun" with Torri—by mutual agreement and understanding, we knew it really wasn't just a game. Along with Edith Piaf, I have no regrets.

What I do regret was that I lived in an era of "the girlfriend"—and not, as was the case for my own children, of simply "girl friends." Over the years, I was blessed with many wonderful girl friends, but, as I page through my old yearbooks, I regret that I did not take the opportunity to make better friends with many of the remarkable women in my school.

In many ways, not just those associated with girls, the early fifties was a pleasant time now buried deep in happy memory. The school doors were open and everybody had a locker stuffed with books and coats. One walked the halls in complete safety. The only fear was getting to class on time. The only smoke in the restroom was from a Pall Mall or a Chesterfield, and coke came in a bottle. If you wanted to see a girl with a tattoo, you had to go to a carnival. The most daring thing we guys did was to guzzle an occasional Schlitz or Old Style Lager, or drive ten or fifteen miles per hour over the speed limit on North Avenue.

Nineteen fifty four marked the beginning of a new era—although we didn't know it at the time. It was the beginning of rock and roll. Congress added "under God" to the pledge of allegiance. And the Supreme Court handed down its landmark school desegregation decision in *Brown v. the Board of Education*. It was truly a time of increasing and momentous changes.

I spent the next seven years in two particularly male institutions: Princeton University and the US Navy. Princeton was still an all-male university, and true to F. Scott Fitzgerald's observations as "the pleasantest country club in America." The navy was an extension of 1950s college life: a male-only institution, characterized by hard work, plenty of liquor and tobacco, but few chances to find and develop good relationships with women. Pat often said the reason I fell for her the first year of law school was that after four years at Princeton and three years in the navy, I couldn't stand coeducation.

During those seven years there had been many girls, some special women, and a few ladies; as the song says, some yeses, some nos, and some maybes. There were several serious relationships. For two years at Princeton, I devoted much of my energy to Helen Lofquist, a beautiful, blond Chicago girl, who attended Lawrence College in Appleton, Wisconsin. While in the navy, I met and chased after another very cute blond from Virginia Beach, Lloyd Tilton, a Mary Washington College student. I guess I had a thing for blonds. Anyway, neither of these romances lasted, for various reasons, not the least of which was time and distance. Someone once said that time and distance are to a love affair like water is to a fire: a little bit makes it sizzle, but too much puts it out.

———

In 1961, as I turned twenty-five, I decided to turn down the US Foreign Service and instead head off to Harvard Law School. My three years of active duty in the US Navy had been good ones, but neither the navy nor another government organization based on bureaucracy and structure appealed to me enough for a life-career commitment. Law school promised another option and opened up new opportunities.

For the summer of 1961, I had been lucky to obtain a job with my old friends at the American Field Service. I had been an AFS summer exchange student in 1953 and had kept in contact with some of the staff in New York. I was hired to be a staff director, aka a counselor/chaperone, on that summer's cruises, going over to Europe with the American students in June and returning with the European kids in August.

On the way over, there were only two male staff: myself and a professor from Michigan. There were several American female staff, but the majority consisted of former European AFSers, mostly women, whose job was to orient the American kids to what they should expect in their various destination countries. Among the staff, I was particularly attracted to Hanna Reichert from Düsseldorf, then studying at University of Cologne. She was smart, attractive, radiant. She wasn't particularly tall, her physique average, but her eyes sparkled, her hair shown, and her smile would have launched the proverbial thousand ships of Troy. With a drop of 4711 Kolnisch Wasser behind her ears and on her neck, she was irresistible. And, she loved Beethoven. We became great friends, shared many Beck's beers, and spent nights on deck, gazing at the stars and talking.

Later that summer I visited her in Düsseldorf—twice. I even sent her a dozen red roses. But it was clear that Hanna didn't see where any of this could go, since I, this crazy American, was going back to the United States to attend law school in the fall.

Theodore Geisel, aka Dr. Seuss, once said, "Don't cry because it's over. Smile because it happened." When I drink a Beck's or smell 4711 or hear Beethoven's Ninth Symphony, I think of Hanna. And, when I think of Hanna, I smile.

The major portion of my summer of '61 was spent in Vienna, where I enrolled in a summer German language course at the university: *Deutsch Sprachkurse für Ausländers.*

After six weeks in Vienna, I had arranged to meet up with my old navy buddy Chuck Carpenter in Mainz. He had gotten out of the navy in June, as I had, and had been traveling around Europe. We decided to travel up the Rhine to Düsseldorf, where I wanted to see Hanna one more time.

Our trip up the Rhine was broken by a one-night stay in Rudesheim, where we had a wonderful evening on the Drosselgasse, a famous street filled with wine bars. Our evening was enriched by two young, attractive American

college girls—sisters—who seemed quite willing to extend
the pleasures of the night indefinitely—until their mother
arrived on the scene about midnight. She believed—and
probably rightly so—that her daughters were better off
in their hotel than somewhere with two ex-navy officers.
Throwing pebbles against their hotel window and shouting for them to assert their independence probably did
nothing to improve our image in the mother's view. We
retreated—alone—back to the bars, and eventually to our
hotel. The next morning I awoke with one of the worst
wine hangovers ever. Thanks to four aspirins from Chuck
and three or four glasses of water, I survived—and will
always be thankful to Lt. Carpenter for saving my life.

I guess I repaid old Chuck when we got to Düsseldorf.
Hanna suggested that we go to Berlin for the weekend—
the "we" meaning Chuck and me. She said we should stay
at the Free University of Berlin and look up her old AFS
friend Christa Sterneman, who worked for Lufthansa.
We did, and the weekend was memorable: August 13–15,
1961, the weekend the Berlin border was closed and the
wall became a reality, to last for the next twenty-eight
years. Just as the wall fell in 1989, Chuck fell like a ton of
bricks for Christa in 1961. They were married in Boulder
in 1962 and have lived in Colorado ever since. A unity of
freedom and happiness: first for Chuck and Christa, and
eventually, for all Berliners and all Germans.

The right time, the right place, and a special woman:
chance, choice—and luck. For Chuck Carpenter it had
been in Berlin. Perhaps the stars would align for me in
Cambridge, Massachusetts.

CHAPTER 3

# Tough, Tender Pat Schroeder

—Title of the cover article in the February 19, 1989,

Sunday *Denver Post Contemporary* magazine

I first saw Pat at Harkness Commons in September of 1961. During the first week at Harvard Law School, the Ames law clubs hold cocktail parties to recruit first year (one-L) members. The principal purpose of these clubs—many named after Harvard professors, past and present—was and is to compete in a moot court competition later the next spring, but they also served as social organizations that had dinners or cocktail parties, often at the house of the sponsoring professor.

As with any club system, some clubs were more prestigious and sought after than others. The Harlen Club, named after Supreme Court Justice John Marshall Harlen, was a club that was particularly popular, and its party was packed. As several of us were walking in, a group was just exiting. One person immediately caught my eye, a girl. Now, there were some 530 of us in the Harvard Law School class of 1961, but only twenty were women. This girl merited a long stare. Tall, slender, attractive. A shock of shining brown hair, high cheekbones, a beautiful smile.

And the outfit? A nicely tailored navy skirt, white blouse, and a heavy navy cardigan sweater covered with various national flags.

When one of my friends said, "Oh, that's Pat Scott. She's in my section and seems pretty nice. She's from the University of Minnesota," I wasn't surprised. She looked—and dressed—like a Big Ten coed on her way to a sorority meeting.

Pat and I were not in the same section, and thus we did not have any classes together. Also, neither of us joined the Harlen Club. (Pat became secretary of the Griswold Club, sponsored by our dean, Ernest Griswold, later solicitor general of the United States, and I joined the Kaplan Club, sponsored by civil procedure expert Benjamin Kaplan, later justice of the Massachusetts Supreme Judicial Court. My fellow club mates included future governor and senator Bob Graham of Florida, and my Ames partner was Peter Berle, later commissioner of New York's Department of Environmental Conservation and president of the National Audubon Society.)

When we arrived at Harvard, we all received a booklet called "The Face Book" with pictures and brief descriptions (name, hometown, undergraduate college) of our classmates. Certainly Pat was one of the most attractive women in our class, a vision of fresh sunshine from the midwestern heartland.

One Thursday evening in late October or early November, I was studying in Langdell Library when Pat walked in. She stopped by the table where I was working, apparently looking for a particular law volume up in the stacks. She smiled, and I asked her if I could be of assistance. "Yes," she said, "could you please get a volume down from the top shelf?" I of course did. We chatted quietly for a few minutes, and I then suggested we go out to dinner Saturday. She said, "Great," and we were set for our first date.

We went to a little Italian restaurant down on Beacon Hill in Boston. Although I can't remember the name of the restaurant, my memories of that evening are still vivid—because, as they say, the rest is history. Somehow I knew that this girl—Pat was just twenty-one—was really special. That evening I learned about Pat what many others have learned: she is smart, enthusiastic, and has boundless energy. She is witty and has a great sense of humor. She is charming, personable, self-assured, and well grounded. And, she dresses funny.

It was cold that night, and Pat wore what I referred to as "the rug": a great green shaggy coat that must have come from Sesame Street. Her shapeless light-green dress was something my mother would have worn to a church supper back in downstate Illinois. Fortunately, neither the coat nor the dress could camouflage the beauty, charm, and wit of the inner package they wrapped.

Smart? I'm sure all the women in the Harvard Law School class of 1964 were smart. But Pat was—and is— very smart. She graduated Phi Beta Kappa and magna cum laude from the University of Minnesota—in three years.

Energetic? She worked her way through college by adjusting aircraft losses for aviation insurance companies as an employee of her father's company. Yes, she was a pilot, having earned a private pilot's license when she was eighteen.

Witty, with a sense of humor? She and her brother bought a 1932 Essex and gave it to their parents on their twenty-fifth wedding anniversary.

I think I knew that first evening together in Boston that my life would not be more fulfilling and rewarding and exciting than if I were to spend it with Pat Scott.

And so it has been.

Forty-seven years—and yes, several new coats, including a terrific western wrangler coat that Gene Upshaw, president of the NFL Players Association, tried to buy off Pat's back on a plane trip to Denver—later, life has never been boring.

Somebody once said, "Don't live with the brakes on." We haven't. The years do go by, perhaps more quickly as we get older, but why slow down when there is always more to see and to do? At the end of life's journey, I suspect that we will not regret what we did but what we did *not* do.

Pat had a remarkable twenty-four-year congressional career (1973–1997) that made her one of the best-known women in American politics, a hero to legions of liberals who admired her uncompromising championship of underdog causes and delighted in her ability to deflate conservative opponents with her stinging wit. She was a trailblazer, a mentor to many other congresswomen, and one of the first women to push against the glass ceiling that Hillary Clinton shattered in 2008.

It has now been twelve years since Pat left Congress, in January 1997. As we travel, however, the same event invariably happens, as it did all within the space of one month in 2005 in the lobby of The Breakers hotel in Palm Beach, walking down a street in Key West, in the Amsterdam airport, and outside a hotel in Oslo, Norway. A woman will stop Pat and say, "Aren't you Pat Schroeder? You've always been one of my heroes. Thank you for all you did for women. We really miss you and need you." If they have a camera, they want to take a picture, or better yet, have me take their picture with Pat.

What is more interesting, perhaps, is that the people who stop Pat—and some are men—are usually not from Denver, or even Colorado. They are from California, Ohio, New York, Massachusetts, or even overseas. When we were waiting for a plane in February 2004, in Lima, Peru, Pat was accosted by a number of people who recognized her and wanted to talk politics. They were Brits waiting for their flight back to the United Kingdom.

One other interesting footnote: About half of the people who come over and speak to Pat call her "senator." She is not only remembered; she's promoted!

And then there are the stories from friends and colleagues. At a Key West conference on Harry Truman in 2005, former US ambassador Bill Brown brought back a lot of memories of an Armed Services Committee Congressional Delegation (CODEL) trip to Moscow in about 1980.

The members of the delegation had been invited to meet with the chairman of the Russian general staff, Marshal Nikolai V. Ogarkov, in the Kremlin. Bill Brown, then political officer at our embassy, had gone to great lengths to arrange the meeting, which was held with the marshal, his staff, and the members of the delegation in a secure room.

Outside, in an ornate Kremlin banquet hall, an elaborate reception had been set up around a massive table covered with food. A hundred or more "nonprincipals" awaited the end of the meeting and the opening of the vodka bottles. As I chatted with Bill Brown, the doors opened and the participants emerged, looking rather serious and heading for the food and drink—but where was Pat?

Then, after about five or ten minutes, the conversations died down and many heads turned, looking down the ornate hallway as Pat and Marshal Ogarkov emerged from another door and walked toward the reception. I asked Brown why everybody had stopped and was staring down the hallway. Bill shook his head and said, "Ogarkov's laughing. Nobody has ever seen him laugh before."

And why was the marshal laughing? Through an interpreter, Ogarkov said that he and Mrs. Schroeder had been discussing the matter of the Jewish refusenics and Mrs. Schroeder said that if he would let Sharansky go, she would be happy to stay in Russia. The marshal said he thought that was very funny.

Natan Sharansky was, at that time, one of the most prominent Jewish dissidents being denied an exit visa. Arrested in 1977, he was finally released in 1986, immigrated to Israel, and became a minister in the Israeli government. Although the Armed Services Committee was not interested in the issue, Pat and Representative Henry Waxman—not a member of the committee, though he had hitched a ride with the CODEL—were. We met with

Sharansky's mother, Ida Milgrom; Ida Nudel; Vladimir Slepak; and many other Jewish dissidents. Compassion and a sense of humor were always part of Pat's stock-in-trade, and in this case, as in many others, they served her well.

Bill Brown became US ambassador to Israel in the 1980s, and his remarks to the Truman Conference in 2005 included several stories about key meetings with Shimon Peres, former defense minister, foreign minister, prime minister, and in the spring of 2007, president of Israel. Pat first met Peres in Israel in 1973.

I can't remember why now, but at some point many years ago, I needed to get something out of my wife's purse. Very dangerous. Snugged down at the bottom among the hairpins, pens, and Kleenex tissues were several business cards held together with a paper clip. The one on top was for Joe, the Balloon Man. One of Pat's favorite things was to order up balloons for our children's birthdays, especially embarrassing them as they got older and the deliveries took place at college or work.

On the back of the card was Shimon Peres's private, direct-line phone number, written in his own hand.

A small thing—a calling card with two important numbers—said a great deal about Pat Schroeder. A sense of humor, fun, and the importance of family: keep Joe's card handy. A desire to work for peace and justice in the Middle East: keep Shimon's number available. Tender and tough Pat Schroeder.

# PART II
# Success Comes in Many Forms

Mensch tracht, un Gott lacht

*(Man plans, God laughs)*

—Yiddish proverb

## CHAPTER 4

# Two Careers: Avoid Competition and Be Prepared to Compromise

*Compromise…is not an eroding of principle
for the sake of getting something done, but a
principle in itself—the certainty of uncertainty,
a basic part of union.*

—Colin Rule, speaking of President Barack Obama
on the Stanford University Center for
Internet and Society website

Having married a fellow law student after our first year of law school, it was certainly my expectation that Pat and I would both complete two more years of study, graduate, then pass a state bar exam, be admitted to practice and practice law—or use our law degrees in some professional manner. It would have been no surprise if we both pursued professional careers. We could anticipate dual careers and begin to think about how we could, and would, handle it.

But I was never really sure that Pat wanted to practice law. When, in our second year, we had the chance to elect some nonrequired courses, Pat chose a comparison course in American and Soviet law while yours truly opted for

Economic Regulation of Business. I accused her of being in the "BA law program" and suggested that she probably would have been happier at Yale. (In those days, real lawyers went to Harvard. Yale was regarded as a good school for those who wanted a law degree but really weren't interested in practicing law.)

I, of course, was more than grateful that Pat had ended up in Cambridge and not New Haven. Married lawyers did present a problem, however, when we started job interviews.

Many law firms send a partner out to various law schools in the spring to conduct job interviews, seeking to hire summer law clerks who could then be offered associate positions upon graduation. The key, then, is that spring interview during your second year.

I had a great interview with John McGrory, the head of Cargill's legal department in Minneapolis, and was offered a summer job. Cargill was—and still is—one of America's largest private corporations, a major grain and food company that also runs a large fleet of barges and vessels. McGrory was a power in Minnesota politics in the 1960s and was chairman of the Third District Republican Party, which included Minneapolis. As a navy veteran from the Midwest, a Republican (yes, I was then still a Republican), and with a wife who had graduated from the University of Minnesota, I seemed to be just what Cargill was looking for.

Well, there was a problem. My new wife—"my gopher," as University of Minnesota alumni are affectionately known—said, "No way! After three years of Minnesota winters, I've had enough." It was my first lesson in compromise.

We turned our attention to other opportunities, particularly to Denver, where Pat's father had an aircraft insurance company.

Few Denver law firms participated in the summer law clerk interview process in the early 1960s. Denver was still somewhat of a backwater, dominated by old-line family firms that were all small by East Coast standards. Davis, Graham & Stubbs, where Supreme Court Justice Byron "Whizzer" White had practiced, did play in the big leagues and sent one of its partners, Don Hoagland, back to Harvard in the spring of 1963. Pat and I both signed up for interviews.

Both Don and the Davis firm were impressive. I think Pat and I had good interviews, but there was a problem. As Don Hoagland explained, Denver was still a small town with a limited legal community. He was concerned about a husband and wife practicing in competing law firms. He felt that Davis, Graham would have to hire both of us or neither of us. As it turned out, the firm's choice was the latter.

Pat and I have subsequently laughed at this experience, especially with Don Hoagland, who became a longtime friend of the Schroeders, as did his talented wife, Mary. In fact, Mary went back to school, obtained a law degree, and became a successful Denver lawyer in her own right.

The fact was, in the early 1960s there were very few women lawyers in Denver: no women partners in any of the major law firms, and only one woman partner, period, who practiced with her brother.

We both interviewed with firms from other cities. Neither of us was particularly interested in living in New

York or Boston, or in California. All other things being equal, which they never are, I would have been happy going back to Chicago, but Pat was not thrilled with the Midwest (she grew up in Hamilton, Ohio, and Des Moines, and didn't want to return to the Midwest). We were both intrigued with Denver and thought we would give it a try—even without firm offers. So in the summer of 1963, we headed west. We had honeymooned in Estes Park and Aspen after our wedding in August 1962, and Pat's dad had bought a house in Thornton, just north of Denver, where we could live.

Pat worked with her father's aviation insurance companies, and I clerked with several independent lawyers— including Arthur Bowman, a former municipal judge; state senator Ed Byrne; Jim Geissinger, a water law expert; and Ben Wright, who specialized in mining law—in the Equitable Building on Seventeenth Street. It was a great introduction to Colorado law.

Upon graduation in 1964, Pat and I returned to Denver and took a Colorado bar refresher course before taking and then passing the Colorado bar exams.

In the end, Pat actually got a permanent job before I did: she was hired by the federal government as a field attorney for the regional office of the National Labor Relations Board (NLRB), covering Colorado, Utah, and Wyoming. I returned to my friends at the Equitable Building while I investigated, and then interviewed with, a number of small to midsized Denver law firms. Fred Winner, one of Denver's finest trial lawyers and later a legendary federal district judge, suggested I talk to Jack Tweedy. Winner thought Tweedy was one of Denver's best business lawyers and his modest-sized firm might be looking for additional lawyers. Tweedy Mosley Sullivan & Young represented not only Vail Associates, developers of the Vail ski area (Jack Tweedy was the lawyer who put Vail together), but also The Oil Shale Corporation (TOSCO), which was then at the forefront of the effort to develop an oil shale industry in Colorado.

I joined Tweedy, Mosley in 1965, subsequently became a partner, and when I left the firm at the end of 1972 after Pat's election to Congress, the firm was known as Mosley, Wells & Schroeder.

It was a great firm, and my years of Denver practice were deeply rewarding. I was privileged to work with some exceptional lawyers and wonderful people and to participate in a remarkable variety of interesting and important legal work.

Floyd Haskell became counsel to our firm in 1968 or 1969. A former Republican state representative and senior partner of his own firm, Floyd left the Republican Party in 1970 after the bombing of Cambodia. In 1972 he became the Democratic candidate for the US Senate against the incumbent, Senator Gordon Allott, then the third ranking senator in the Republican Party. I started out as Floyd's temporary campaign manager, and when he announced his entry into the race in April 1972, Pat helped me pick up coffee and donuts on South Broadway for the press conference.

Less than a month later, I told Floyd that I couldn't continue with his campaign because I was joining another one: my wife's.

So if your spouse is a lawyer, you can expect that she will want to use her degree to practice law, to work in business, or perhaps to teach. However, she may change directions, as Pat did, from government practice to teaching to private practice and then back to public service. She may even run for public office—and win.

———

Whatever problems there are for two-career couples—and, of course, there are problems—they are probably fewer if both people have careers in the same area. When I would tell someone that my wife was a lawyer, the reaction was often, "Oh, that must be great; you can discuss your cases and understand each other." Well, that was the last thing I had in mind, and I suspect Pat felt the same way. After a hard day at the office, who wants to come home and talk shop, even to a fellow shopkeeper?

It is an advantage in this respect: if your spouse really knows what your job entails, what its demands and pressures are, he or she is more likely to understand, appreciate, and accept those demands and pressures. When Saturday at the mall followed by a quiet dinner and movie gets cancelled due to a weekend all-nighter at the office because a brief must be filed in court on Monday morning, a lawyer spouse may be more sympathetic than a nonlawyer spouse.

I am sure the same thing is true in other professions. The physician married to a nurse practitioner or psychiatric social worker may get a more knowing nod and smile as she hurries out to an evening hospital emergency. A member of the military who is ordered to move out in forty-eight hours is likely to get more understanding from a fellow military spouse or a spouse who has experienced the demands of a military career.

My son, Scott, and his wife, Amy, are both Columbia MBAs. They both worked at American Express. Scott is now with Dunn & Bradstreet, and Amy, now with young twins at home, still consults with Amex three days a week and has several other clients. They both know the pressures of the credit card business, the demands of financial and strategic planning, the deadlines of marketing. So far, they are surviving well—in large measure, I believe, because they understand and accept the limitations placed on each other by their jobs.

My daughter, Jamie, and her husband, Neil Cornish, are somewhat different. Both are PhD's: Jamie in education and Neil in astrophysics. Jamie wrote her thesis comparing children's television in the United Kingdom and the United States. She is now marketing and public affairs director for the Museum of the Rockies in Bozeman, Montana. Neil teaches at Montana State University in Bozeman, is a member of NASA's science advisory team, and also a consultant to the European Space Agency. Neil is concerned with the shape and age of the universe. Jamie is concerned with the shape and development of children's minds.

But they try to understand and appreciate the pressures and demands of each other's jobs. Often, those pressures and demands are the same: budgets and recruiting and keeping good people, whether students, staff, or colleagues.

———

Now we get to the big questions. Over the years, I have most often been asked two things: How does it feel to be married to Pat Schroeder? and How do you handle the fact that your wife is more successful and important than you are?

Inherent in such questions is the assumption that a man is supposed to be the predominant partner in any two-career relationship and that the male ego cannot cope with a more successful spouse. Frankly, I've always been amused by this proposition. I eventually realized, however, that it's a real issue. It especially came home to me when I noticed how many young women reporters seemed to be fascinated by the fact that I was not threatened by my wife's prominence or jealous of her position and success. Pursuing careers of their own, they were eager to learn how I did it: How did I handle it? Were there men who could survive playing second fiddle to a woman? Could a man subordinate himself and his career to his partner?

I think it all goes back to competition, and to the essence of a productive and meaningful partnership. Being a lawyer—and, of course, my wife is a lawyer too—I think I have gained some insight into these issues of competition and partnership.

First, competition.

One day, while driving back to Orlando, I was listening to National Public Radio and heard an interview of an author of a new book on the subject of female competition. I've forgotten her name, and even the title of her book, but it was something about cat fights, which illustrates her point of view: girls are not raised in the same competitive atmosphere as boys and therefore have more trouble handling competitive situations, especially with other women. Hence, women are often the worst critics of other successful women and do not know how to respond to, let alone encourage or support, other women. Professor Cathy Tinsley of Georgetown University's McDonough School of Business and executive director of the Georgetown Women's Leadership Initiative has observed that women are perhaps the only "low-status" group whose members systematically and harshly show prejudice toward fellow members. I recall that when my wife was exploring running for president in 1987, her toughest and most strident critics seemed to be women.

But what I really want to discuss is competition *between* men and women, especially between partners or spouses who are also colleagues. I submit that in this case, competition doesn't work: for a successful and happy relationship, a man and woman cannot be competitors. One need only look to Hollywood and the failure of one marriage after another. You simply cannot be consumed by your own career and success—and concerned primarily with your star burning brighter than your spouse's—and maintain a stable and rewarding partnership. As Hollywood star Amy Adams observed about her six-year relationship with her actor boyfriend and fiancé Darren Le Gallo, "He's not competitive with me; he does not think that my success is his failure."

When Pat and I started law school in the fall of 1961, there was one married couple in our class, Jim and Diana Lorenz, both extremely bright, intelligent, and attractive people. They graduated and became quite successful—Jim as a lawyer, labor organizer, government official, and author in California, Diana a successful lawyer and academic—but not together. Their marriage failed soon after they left law school. And, I think, one could see why: they were always competing with each other.

My good Princeton and navy buddy Jon Masters and I, however, married classmates after our first year and remain happily married.

Now, it's not because Jon and I are pieces of milquetoast or hate competition. We are, if I may say, regular guys who love a good party and love competition: witness the Lincoln's Inn Society dinner in 1963, when we inflicted some damage upon the Hasty Pudding Club in a fit of alcoholic exuberance. We have had successful legal careers, and we have had fun. What we have not done is compete against our wives. There is a line in the last chapter of a book I just read, *The Tenth Justice*, about two Supreme Court clerks, one male, one female, that says it all: "That's the problem with competitive friendships— they shatter at the slightest impact."

People used to ask me who got higher grades, or who had a higher class standing, or who received a job offer first, or who made more money. My answer was the same as Jon's: either I didn't know, or I didn't particularly care. Jon's objective was to support Rosemary and help her with whatever professional path she chose to follow. Likewise, I wanted Pat to use her degree however and wherever she chose. Rosemary and Pat also encouraged Jon and me to follow our own lights. As couples we were, in a word, teammates. Our successes or failures were to come together, not apart from or at the expense of, the other.

The best reward is not to win the game yourself, especially at a high cost to your integrity or relationships, but to play the game unselfishly and to the best of your ability, to contribute to and support a successful team effort. When your teammate happens to be your wife, you will probably win a lot more games than you'll lose!

So don't put a scoreboard over your back door labeled His and Hers. Instead of keeping score, keep a sense of perspective, balance, and luck. I recommend a horseshoe. Or a mezuzah.

Which leads me to partnerships.

After all—and above all—marriage is a partnership. Law firms, too, are traditionally founded and exist upon the highest principles of partnership. Partners are independent, often strong-willed individuals who come together in the hope and expectation of building something stronger and better together. They must trust and respect each other and become fiduciaries: each can in fact bind and act for the partnership. They can, and do, continue to act for themselves, but they have a responsibility and obligation to work for the greater good of the partnership. Often that means that one's own personal views or desires need to be moderated or adjusted, or even subordinated, to the will of the other partner or the partnership. You can't always have your own way—certainly in a law firm partnership, and most definitely in a marriage.

So I didn't take that job offer from Cargill. Incidentally, that's one of Pat's problems: she hates cold weather. When my Denver law firm asked me to open up the first law office in Vail, Pat's reply was the same: "No way!"

So Pat and I went to Denver, and we stayed in Denver. And the people of Denver were subsequently blessed with twenty-four years of outstanding and exciting representation in the US Congress.

———

Now let me turn to some thoughts about compromise.

An experienced lawyer knows that a good settlement is better than a bad lawsuit. A winning case can be lost because of an unsympathetic jury or a judge's faulty ruling. Losing cases are often won, but probably against the odds, and lawyers, like gamblers, need to play by the odds. In the immortal words of Kenny Rogers, "You got to know when to hold 'em, know when to fold 'em, know when to walk away, and know when to run."

Smart businessmen also learn that compromise may be the best strategy. Should I continue to throw good money after bad? Why not put this matter behind us, learn from the experience, and move forward? Half a loaf is better than none.

We all negotiate our way through life. We may stand on principle and refuse to budge. But more often than not, the reasonable course of action is to compromise, to give up something in order to achieve something else—or, for that matter, anything at all.

There is, however, a problem with compromises. If one person says 100 and another 0, a compromise at 50–50 or 60–40 may be achieved and be satisfactory to both. But what if the "compromise" is 90–10? In other words, one party compromises—or surrenders—totally. He or she hears, "It's my way, or the highway," and to avoid the highway, gives in to the other.

When one party always seems to end up with the short end of the stick, or worse, surrenders completely, the prospects for a relationship that will continue to survive and develop positively appear dim.

———

The great German chancellor Otto Von Bismark once observed that "Politics is the art of the possible." A good politician or statesman knows when compromise is possible and necessary to move forward a legislative agenda and actively accomplish something. As an example, Pat first introduced a parental and medical leave bill in 1985 with no cosponsors. When it finally passed the Congress in 1990, it had been substantially modified from its original version, but President George H. W. Bush vetoed it anyway. When the bill passed in Congress again in the fall of 1992, Bush vetoed it a second time. Although the Senate voted to override the veto, the House vote fell short.

Family and medical leave became a major issue in the 1992 presidential campaign. After Bill Clinton won the election, his administration called for speedy action, and Congress responded. On February 5, 1993, Clinton signed the Family and Medical Leave Act, the first bill he signed as president. It was a victory for compromise and for Pat—for her years of tireless work and dedicated effort.

Most importantly, though, it was a victory for America's working families.

Pat's ability to compromise as a politician was matched by her ability to compromise within our marriage. For example, I love opera and am a member of the board of trustees of the Orlando Opera. Musical comedy is not my favorite, but it is Pat's. The compromise here is easy. When we are in New York for a weekend, we will often spend one night at the Metropolitan Opera and one on Broadway.

And, guess what? We have both grown and enjoyed different and new experiences. I think Pat now looks forward to a great Verdi opera as much as I do. And I did like *Phantom of the Opera*. I've even seen it four times. (Pat says I had to because I fell asleep during various portions of the first three performances.)

Cooperation. Compromises. Every family, and particularly every two-career family, knows what I'm talking about. Circumstances change. Adjustments have to be made.

———

I think there are two major realities that every dual-career couple must face. At any particular time, or perhaps all the time, one career may be the dominant or leading one. The partner with the secondary or less prominent career will probably be the one faced with making more compromises or accommodations. Historically, it was the man's career that was the principal one, but that is not necessarily so today, and it was not in our case, at least after Pat was elected to Congress.

Second, if and when children enter the picture, it is inevitable—and I think necessary—that the wife will assume greater responsibility and require more time and effort with the children and on the home front than the husband. The responsibilities and joys of parenthood can and should be shared, but I am sure Pat—and Jamie and Amy—would agree that the burdens are not equal. Yes, I did help, and Neil and Scott do better and far more than I ever did. The ladies can't and should not have to do it all. But they will do more. Their career paths will therefore be subject to different pressures and choices.

After Scott was born in 1966, Pat decided not to return to her full-time job at the NLRB, instead seeking work that would be professionally rewarding but give her more flexibility and her own time. Private law practice was difficult to conduct from home, although she did eventually become counsel to Rocky Mountain Planned Parenthood. From 1969 to 1970 she became a lecturer and law instructor at the Community College of Denver and the University of Colorado at Denver. Our daughter Jamie was born in 1970.

From 1970 through 1972, Pat taught at Regis College, a Jesuit school in north Denver. During her years in Congress, we were always invited to dinner with the presidents of the Jesuit colleges when they would meet in Washington. We had many close friends among this group, including Father Healey and later Father O'Donovan of Georgetown, where our son, Scott, went to college. Although a leading feminist, Pat was welcomed by this distinguished group of Catholic leaders because of mutual concerns about the issues of higher education, poverty, and foreign and military policy, such as the troubles in Central American in the 1980s.

From 1971 to 1972, Pat served as a hearing officer for the Colorado Department of Personnel and Administration.

Upon reflection, all of these positions added to Pat's personal and professional growth, and increased her knowledge about and visibility within a variety of important Denver communities, as well as allowing her the freedom to spend more time with our children during their early childhood years. If she had been planning to run for public office, which she wasn't, she couldn't have done much better. A series of minor, seemingly unconnected choices can often lay a solid foundation for seizing a major opportunity when it eventually comes along.

———

When opportunity knocks on the door of a married couple, both may open it, but only one may be able to walk out that door and down a new path—hopefully with the encouragement and support of the other. For years people asked me why I didn't run for Congress in 1972. The short and best answer is that I, and others, decided we needed a stronger candidate, and we were able to convince Pat that she should run. The long answer is somewhat more complicated.

In 1970, I had run for the Colorado state legislature and lost by forty-two votes, still one of the closest races in Colorado history. I ran in a traditionally Republican, eastside Denver district, and therefore, it was a moral victory of sorts.

The Republicans then made a mistake, overreaching, as they are often prone to do. Following the 1970 Census, the legislature redrew the district boundaries, and somehow my precinct—the only precinct lying south of Colfax Avenue, Denver's major east-west highway—was put into a district lying north of Colfax. This district was traditionally Democratic, but it was also the heart of Denver's minority population and already represented by a young black lawyer named Wellington Webb, later to become mayor of Denver and a vice chairman of the 2004 Democratic National Convention, held in Boston. I couldn't run against Wellington, and I didn't want to.

The other thing the Republican legislature did was to redraw the congressional district lines. In the hope of making Denver's First District more friendly for their new Republican incumbent, Congressman Mike McKevitt, they moved a number of traditionally Democratic Denver west side precincts into the suburban Second District. This would presumably help in McKevitt's 1972 reelection efforts and not hurt the Republican incumbent too much in the Second District.

This strategy, of course, didn't work. Pat was able to win back the First District in 1972, and again in 1974, in the aftermath of Watergate. With the help of those Denver west side precincts, Tim Wirth was able to win the Second District.

But back to 1972.

My primary political efforts in 1972 were to work for my law partner Floyd Haskell's election to the US Senate. I was also a Denver Democratic district precinct captain and among a small group of political activists looking for a candidate for the First Congressional District. It was not proving to be easy.

First, the Democratic Party in Denver was still split between the Humphrey-Labor wing and the McGovern-Kennedy wing, and also over the Vietnam War. Second, the incumbent, Mike McKevitt, Denver's former district attorney, was the second most popular Republican in the Denver metropolitan area, trailing only Governor John Love. Third, another strong Democrat was in the running, the state senate Democratic leader Arch Decker, but he thought the war in Vietnam was just great. Accordingly, it looked like a lost cause for a liberal, and the potential candidates we approached—a state senator, a state representative, a Hispanic judge—were not interested in becoming a sacrificial lamb.

The group decided we still needed a good candidate, someone to carry on the liberal anti-Vietnam, pro–civil rights, and environmental banners. So one night at a late meeting, my fellow conspirators announced, "We think we need a woman. How about your wife?" (I said to Larry Wright, who later worked for Pat in her congressional office, "How about your wife?")

The simple fact was that Pat was a great potential choice: she was uniquely qualified to unite the Democratic Party, to appeal to independent voters, and to energize younger voters, especially women. She was smart and energetic, she was right on the tough issues, and she was attractive, popular, and likeable.

I urged Pat to run. I was confident that we could juggle

our lives for six months and that the kids would survive and benefit from the experience, and even enjoy the excitement. I knew that the campaign would be an exciting, educational, important, and necessary political effort both for the Denver Democratic Party and the country at large. It probably would be, however, a Stevensonian campaign: talk sense to the American people—and lose. I had written my senior thesis at Princeton on Adlai Stevenson's governorship of Illinois. I had also read most of his speeches from the 1952 and 1956 presidential campaigns and had met with and interviewed Stevenson in Chicago. Those races against Dwight Eisenhower carried very long odds and were unsuccessful. Pat's 1972 challenge to a popular Republican incumbent congressman, with the prospect of negative coattails from George McGovern at the top of the ticket, promised to end the same way.

Yet even with those long odds, Pat became an exceptional candidate and ran a brilliant campaign, conceived and managed in large part by two young Denver advertising executives, Arnie Grossman and Chuck Bartholomew.

I didn't act as Pat's campaign manager, but I did offer suggestions on strategy and tactics. I also was active in fund-raising. As many traditional sources of support were not available in a primary contest (Pat beat Decker hardily), I advanced the campaign $25,000 in order to get the race under way. The loan, of course, was paid off, as Pat's contributions—at the average rate of $7.50!—eventually came rolling in.

Even up until the weekend before the election, I still believed I would be back at my Denver law practice the next week and our lives would get back to normal. Then, three things happened that Saturday morning that got me thinking about the previously unimaginable.

First, we received a report on the latest *Denver Post* poll, which would be published in Sunday's paper. It showed that Democrats were uniting behind Pat, that she was doing well with independents, and that she was even picking up some Republicans. She was now running only 4 percent behind McKevitt, with less than 12 percent undecided. Polls are primarily important to show movement, and Pat was gaining on the incumbent.

Second, I answered a knock at our back door, and who should it be but Lauren Watson, head of the Black Panthers in Denver, with some of his fellow members. He'd come to pick up campaign literature for a final door-to-door drop in Denver's traditionally black neighborhoods. If Lauren was in charge, you knew the literature would be delivered, and his efforts boded well for a strong Democratic turnout at the polls on Tuesday.

Finally, as I was giving Lauren his bundles of flyers the phone rang, and it was Wilber Mills, calling from Little Rock, Arkansas. Congressman Wilber Mills, chairman of the House Committee on Ways and Means and one of the most powerful men in the Congress. Wilber just wanted to call and wish Pat good luck. His wife had taken a particular interest in Pat's race. Well, if Wilber Mills was calling, it had to mean that some Washington politicos saw Pat as a potential winner.

Saturday's signs did accurately foretell the future. On that November Tuesday in 1972, Pat became the first woman elected to Congress from the State of Colorado; one of only a few Democratic challengers to beat a Republican incumbent in 1972, defeating McKevitt 52 percent to 48 percent; and at thirty-two, the second youngest woman ever elected to Congress.

By the way, the House Ways and Means Committee was also the Democratic Committee on Committees. Chairman Wilber Mills was critically important in securing a seat on the House Armed Services Committee for Pat—the first woman to serve on that committee—over the strong objections of its chairman, Mr. F. Edward Hébert.

As with any two-career family, events occur that change the dynamic between the two partners. My wife had been elected to the US Congress. Suddenly, her job, her position, her career had catapulted over mine. She had become the primary player in our relationship. In fact, I would soon be out of a job and looking for work. Our children were just two and six years old. Jamie was still in diapers. Over the years, many women came up to me and said, "Oh, how wonderful, you gave up your own career and followed your wife to Washington!"

But I had, after all, encouraged Pat to run. Now that she had won, I felt I had to do all I could to help and support her as she undertook her daunting new responsibilities. Pat certainly had doubts about winning. At one point she joked, "Do I really have to go to Washington?" "Yes," I said, "now that you have been elected, you need to take on and do the job. You can do it, and I'll be with you all the way."

————

I believe Pat's initial congressional pay was $35,000 a year. Both financially and logistically, it would be difficult to maintain two separate households. We were going to need one base, and the logical place for that would be in Washington. (This was 1973, and Congress still worked a full week in Washington. The Tuesday-to-Thursday "do-nothing" Congress of the George W. Bush era was still in the future, and congressional travel budgets for trips home were limited. Unless a congressman represented an East Coast district, it was impractical to try and maintain a primary home in your own state.)

My objectives, then, were to wind up my Denver law firm practice, sever my ties with various civic, business, and community organizations, find a house in the Washington area, get the kids settled into schools, and help Pat set up her congressional office and staff. In due course, I would look for a job.

I did want to find something to do. Becoming a full-time "house husband" had little appeal. And, my political sense told me that once Pat was organized, I should stay out of her congressional affairs and office. There were, and have been, cases where spouses have chosen to work in their husband's or wife's congressional office, but that didn't look like an option for me. All I could see there would be an opportunity to create problems and tensions and a point for obvious criticism.

As a lawyer, I wasn't afraid about finding a job in Washington. As the husband of a newly elected congresswoman, however, the trick would be to find the right job, one that I would be happy with but that would not present problems for Pat.

There is always the possibility of conflicts of interest, both real and perceived, for the two-career family. What if, after Pat had joined the legal staff of the NLRB, I had become counsel to a local labor union? Probably a real conflict of interest. What if Pat had joined a Denver firm that represented the Colorado National Bank and I had joined a competitor firm that represented the United Bank of Denver? If not a real conflict of interest, at least a perceived one, certainly within the local legal and business communities.

When I began looking around Washington in the spring of 1973, my choices seemed to lie in three areas: on Capitol Hill, with another member of Congress or on a congressional committee staff; with a public interest or nonprofit organization; or in private law practice. There were no jobs in the Nixon administration for the husbands of Democratic congresswomen. Likewise, the private business sector was unlikely to take much interest in someone who might only be around for another eighteen months and was primarily interested in having flexibility and time versus the responsibility and salary of a 24/7 commitment.

As for the Hill, I talked with a number of friends who worked there, and they confirmed that it would be difficult if not impossible for me, as Pat's husband, to fit in comfortably on the staff of a senator or another member of Congress.

I talked with several public interest organizations, including Ralph Nader's. A fellow law school classmate,

Alan Morrison, was heading up Nader's litigation group. Then I thought, "Sure that's what Pat really needs, for me to join up with some group whose principal mission is to criticize or even sue Congress! I don't think so."

Clearly, the best route for me appeared to be to rejoin the private practice of law. But there would be constraints. I really was more interested in my time and having flexibility than in making the most money possible. Moreover, I wanted to avoid the all-too-common Washington law practice of lobbying and influence peddling. I wanted independence, the ability to pick and choose the clients I represented and the types of cases I'd be working for. Finally, I had to be honest: in less than two years, we could be headed back to Denver. The first election may be the toughest, but the second is the one that tells you whether that initial victory was a fluke or for real.

Although I had former classmates or contacts at a number of Washington firms, the firm that particularly interested me was Kirkwood, Kaplan, Russin & Vecchi (KKRV). The firm was unique because it had offices and partners in a number of foreign countries—Thailand, Indonesia, Lebanon, Colombia, South Vietnam, the Dominican Republic—and specialized in international public and private law matters.

A close friend and law school classmate, Al Chandler, was a partner in Bangkok, and Pat and I had visited the firm's Bogotá office on a trip to Colombia in 1970. I had also recently worked with Jay Kaplan, one of the firms name partners, on a matter involving Colorado.

KKRV was handling an interesting case. Colonel John

Paul Vann, the legendary Vietnam advisor and warrior, had died in a helicopter crash in Vietnam in the summer of 1972. In 1971, Vann had been divorced by his longtime wife, who lived with their children in Littleton, Colorado. Vann, however, had a Vietnamese "wife" and daughter in Saigon. In April of 1972, after surviving another brush with death in a helicopter crash, Vann had pulled out a notepad and handwritten a short will, leaving all his estate to "my wife, X, and my daughter, X," his Vietnamese family.

After Vann's death, his life insurance and various pensions made up an estate worth fighting over. His Colorado wife sought to annul the earlier divorce and rely on a will Vann had executed and filed in Colorado in 1968. KKRV represented the Vietnamese wife and daughter, and the issue became the legality and standing of a holographic, or handwritten, will under Colorado law.

To make a long story short, the Vietnamese family won. But, I thought, if this is the type of cases these people get involved in, it sounds like the kind of firm where I would really enjoy working. (KKRV continued to represent the Vietnamese family, and I worked with award-winning correspondent Neil Sheehan on royalty issues involving *A Bright Shining Lie*, a book he'd written about Vann, as well as the subsequent HBO movie. Neil was not only a talented writer and courageous correspondent, but also an honorable and sensitive human being.)

I had lunch with Charles Kirkwood, who had founded KKRV, on July 4, 1966, in Bangkok. After discussing my interests and concerns about reentering private law practice, Charlie said he thought we would make a good fit. KKRV had just taken on a new, big case for a Thai company that would probably involve litigation in both Thailand and Washington. They could certainly use some experienced help. I would be treated as a partner, but could work and travel pretty much as I wished. Naturally, my compensation would be tied to my work effort.

By April of 1973, I had found a new home with KKRV in their elegant townhouse offices at 1218 Sixteenth Street NW, Washington, DC. I was off to Bangkok, Thailand, with Charlie on what would be the first of many, many trips to Asia over the next twenty years.

I had found my niche. I would stay off Capitol Hill and out of Pat's congressional office. I would stay away from lobbying. I would pursue a challenging and interesting career in the international law arena. And, I would continue to be careful and to stay out of trouble (most of the time), always mindful that my actions could adversely affect Pat's congressional career. My goal was to continue to do my share at home and with our children, and to support Pat. Looking back, I guess I did a pretty good job. With some hard work, a lot of luck, and the grace of God, anything is possible—even surviving and prospering with the most talented, indefatigable, and witty Pat Schroeder.

CHAPTER 5

# Second Place Isn't Bad
# When Your Wife Is a Winner

*Jim goes to Washington, but his wife's the politician.*
—*Chicago Tribune* headline, March 15, 1973

In our early days together in Denver, I suppose my career was the primary one. When Pat was elected to Congress in November 1972, things certainly changed, and hers became the primary career. This meant that I was faced with making more accommodations, more compromises. In a two-profession home, often one partner has to accept the face of a subordinate role, that their career is secondary.

Should this be a problem, a threat to one's ego? I don't think so. It's just a fact of life. A reality. Certainly for the spouse of a member of Congress.

After the election, we went back to Washington in mid-November for a week of orientation meetings for new members of Congress. At a meeting with the then Speaker of the House, Carl Albert, Speaker Albert grabbed my hand and asked me what committee assignments I was interested in pursuing. When I responded that I was not the new member, that my wife was, he immediately stepped back, turned to Pat—and that's the last I ever saw of Carl Albert.

Several nights later we attended a reception at the State Department for newly elected members. Pat preceded me in the receiving line. A young woman staffer, clipboard in hand, came over and asked if I would go first. In Washington, and at diplomatic functions, she said, the member of Congress or the public official was to be introduced first, not his wife. I explained we were in the right order: Pat was the newly elected member of Congress, not me. She then stepped back and checked her clipboard. Looking up, smiling, she said, "Oh, you're Mr. Pat Schroeder."

Years later I became good friends with Erik Tarloff. A noted screenwriter and accomplished author from Los Angeles, Erik came to Washington in 1993 after President Clinton named Erik's wife, University of California at Berkeley professor Laura Tyson, chair of the President's Council of Economic Advisors. Erik and I appeared on several panels together discussing the life of political husbands, and both of us received a "Good Guy Award," officially know as the Martin Abzug Memorial Award, from the National Women's Political Caucus, Erik in 1994, myself in 1987.

Erik complained that in Washington he went from equal member of a two-career marriage to "also present." He went from being Mr. Tarloff to being Mr. Tyson. I told Erik that I never had that problem. When people called me Mr. Pat Schroeder, I just laughed and said, "Yes, Pat has gone a long way on my name."

Washington is different. Pat used to say that many of the ego problems in Washington were caused by the fact that everyone was constantly reminded by the media that Washington was the most powerful city in the United States and the United States, of course, was the most powerful country in the world. So, if you are a player there, you are powerful and therefore, important.

My own take on Washington can be summed up by the usual conversation that initially occurs at a cocktail party. You walk in, order a drink, and then approach an unattached female who looks like someone who might be interesting to talk to. Based on my experience here is how things might go:

In Denver:

"Hi, my name is Jim Schroeder."

"My name is Sally Smith. Nice to meet you. You look like you've been skiing."

"Yes, I was up at Winter Park on Sunday. The snow was fantastic."

In Chicago or LA:

"Hi, I'm Jim Schroeder."

"I'm Sally Smith. I'm in advertising. What do you do?"

In Washington, DC:

"Hi, my name is Jim Schroeder."

"I'm Sally Smith. I'm staff director of the House Committee on Foreign Affairs. Why are you here?"

No joke. This happened to me over and over again. You are somebody in Washington because of your job. You are at a particular party because you are "a player." That means that somebody else at the party is a player too. You may be a lawyer or a government official. That's almost assumed. The real question is, what is your particular position or distinguishing feature: Why are *you* at *this* party?

In Denver and many other cities, initial cocktail talk will usually be about the weather or sports. In Chicago, LA, or New York, it may be about your job, where you work, what you do. Only in Washington, DC, I submit, is the first question often, "Why are you here?"

When the answer was "Well, I'm here with my wife, Congresswoman Pat Schroeder," the truth was out. I was not a player, and my prospective new acquaintance often moved on while I had another shrimp.

This situation was particularly interesting with lobbyists. Every congressional spouse can recount the experience of being at a Washington cocktail party and being introduced in this way: "I'd like you to meet Jim Schroeder." The lobbyist doesn't know you, he's never met you, and his eyes are focused past your shoulder to the crowd beyond, looking for a familiar, more important face. Then your friend adds, "Jim is Congresswoman Pat Schroeder's husband."

It is as if the lobbyist is hit by lightning. He turns to face you directly, then smiles and pumps your hand. "It's great to meet you. I really admire your wife. Is Pat here? I'd love to chat with her about what happened today on that (fill in the blank) bill."

In the 1970s and 1980s, the Washington social scene operated on several levels. Subsequent changes in ethics and congressional roles have, I think, curtailed some of the practices of these older days, but back then there were the big dinners, two or three thousand people packed into the Shoreham Hotel or the Washington Hilton, for example, for the annual meeting of the American Legion or the VFW. Usually there would be a delegation from Denver, and an appearance by Mrs. Schroeder, a member of the House Armed Services Committee, was expected. Pat would see that I was invited, and we would both attend. Often, especially with smaller affairs, the invitation was only to the member; spouses were not included. Pat often turned down such events since I was not included.

The medium-level Washington social events were all over the lot: political fund-raisers, organizational dinners, honorary testimonials, cultural events—you name it. When I went, I was often relegated to the "cheap seats." While Pat would be seated at the head table or at a table with other luminaries; I would be back near the kitchen with other spouses or staffers. At one dinner, I ended up at a table with Senator Jay Rockefeller's children. Actually, they were great kids and they got a kick out of learning that I was a classmate of their Uncle Steve.

By far the best part of the Washington social scene was the small cocktail or dinner party, eight to ten or twelve but less than twenty, held at a club, embassy, or private home. Here was an opportunity to really talk with and get to know someone, to exchange ideas, learn, and develop an actual friendship. Someone once said that in

Washington, one has many acquaintances but few friends. A smaller, congenial setting offered the opportunity of building real friendships.

Even at these smaller affairs, it was clear that Pat was the star. At an embassy dinner party, Pat would be seated at the right hand of the ambassador. Not always, but often, I would be seated on the other side of the table next to the wife of the political counselor.

Over the years, things did change. My law firm had offices in the Dominican Republic, Thailand, and Taiwan. We were Washington counsel to the Embassy of Israel and represented the governments of India, Pakistan, and Iran in major international business, trade, and litigation matters. I personally handled business and trade matters for Thai, Israeli, and Philippine companies and became involved in a case that had repercussions in Turkey. When we went to dinner at these embassies, I sat next to the ambassador's wife.

The Washington social scene is different from that of other cities. Pleasure is inextricably tied up with position and power. As at any social event, however, if the host and hostess find both partners of a guest couple to be interesting, the chances of a repeat invitation increase substantially. Numerous evenings out at the Canadian Embassy, especially during the tenure of Ambassador Allan Gotlieb, are a good example.

Allan was a successful Canadian lawyer before he became a diplomat. His wife, Sondra, was an accomplished writer and author. Pat was a welcome guest at the Canadian Embassy. As fellow lawyers interested in international trade matters and as devout hockey fans, Allan and I always enjoyed good conversations, particularly in his book-filled study in the company of some excellent Havana cigars.

Sondra and I also hit it off. Attractive, feisty, and independent, she enjoyed exchanging stories about our roles as second bananas.

So the Schroeders were frequent guests at the Canadian Embassy and at many Canadian government events. One memorable event involved a premiere of a Canadian film, *Black Robe*, by the National Film Board of Canada. The board violated several rules for evening Washington social events: the program started late, the film was too long, and a formal dinner was scheduled *after* the film was over. Successful Washington events start early and on time and end early, so that the power elite can get home and prepare for the next day's busy schedule.

There was, however, a very happy ending to this night, at least for our wonder dog, Wolfie.

Because the Gotliebs were such good friends, we felt we had to attend the post-movie dinner. It was held at a restaurant near the theater, but by the time we sat down, it was after eleven o'clock and half the tables were empty. The main course turned out to be tender, juicy filet mignons, a favorite of Pat's and mine, but a bit heavy for an 11:30 snack before bed.

Pat ate only half her filet. As we were getting ready to leave, she asked our waiter if she could get a doggy bag, saying, "I just can't finish this, and my Keeshond puppy will be very happy when I bring this home."

The waiter smiled and asked if we might like some

extra steaks. Because the dinner had started so late, half the guests had not even shown up, and there were a lot of leftovers. We said yes, and he returned with a big, heavy bag of ten to twelve beautiful filets.

Needless to say, when we returned home, Wolfie went crazy. For the next couple of weeks he dined on the best meat he had ever had. Although a Dutch breed, I thought I detected a slight Canadian accent in his ecstatic bark.

By the way, Harry Truman was right. If you want a true friend in Washington, get a dog.

CHAPTER 6

# My Separate Career

*You are mine and I / am yours in love, /*
*I am I and you are / you in thought.*
*Independently we / share our lives / together.*
—Susan Polis Schutz

The best thing I did in my life was marrying Pat. But probably the next best thing was having a separate career. It enriched my life and our marriage and family life. It did not detract from or become a detriment to Pat's successful political career. We gave each other some space in order to build something solid together.

I would certainly not disparage or criticize the spouse—usually the woman, the traditional housewife and mother—who chooses not to pursue or continue to pursue an independent career. Both my mother and Pat's mother were college graduates who taught grade school before they were married. They never returned to full-time teaching, content with raising families, supporting successful husbands, and pursuing community, civic, and church activities.

Particularly in the political world, the "ideal" spouse may well be one who does *not* have a separate career or, at the least, has given up his or her career to support the political spouse full time. I knew several congressmen and senators whose wives devoted their free time and efforts exclusively to fulfilling the role, duties, and responsibilities—at least as they saw them—of "the wife of the Honorable..."

Frankly, in this regard I thought Pat, and perhaps several other congresswomen, were at a disadvantage; they didn't have political wives ready, willing, and able to stand in for them at political, social, or civic events.

Former Colorado governor Dick Lamm and his wife, Dottie, are longtime friends and political allies. I saw Dottie in action on numerous occasions, often standing in for Dick, and she was terrific. She was so good that the Colorado Democratic Party later nominated her for the US Senate. Unfortunately, she didn't win.

Former Colorado senator Gary Hart was fortunate to have the strong and steady support of his wife, Lee, in his successful Senate races in Colorado and in his less successful efforts running for the Democrat presidential nomination.

Lee was and is tall, attractive, articulate, and smart. In many ways, she seemed more comfortable addressing certain gatherings then Gary did. I think Lee really liked meeting and talking with new people. People seemed interested in meeting her. At one campaign function in Denver, we both ended up subbing for our spouses, who were tied up in Washington. True, it was an event dominated by women, but I distinctly felt that those present were flattered that Lee had come in Gary's absence. They were less certain what to do with me.

In following Pat to Washington, there were the stresses and regrets associated with turning over client work and terminating client and law firm relationships. The more I thought about it, though, the more I realized that I was being presented with an opportunity to change my career path, or at least explore new areas of law practice with a different type of law firm. I wasn't worried about finding a job—after all, Washington probably has more lawyers per capita than any other major US city. Presumably, there were plenty of jobs for lawyers.

The reason for the high concentration of lawyers in Washington, DC, is that Washington is not only the home of Congress, it is the location for the federal executive office departments and numerous independent agencies. As the nation's capital, Washington is the location of many foreign embassies and home to important international organizations, such as the World Bank, the International Finance Corporation, and the International Monetary Fund.

In 1973 I was new to Washington and knew I had no particular experience and less knowledge about the inner workings of Capitol Hill. Any prospective client who approached me for lobbying advice or assistance would probably do so in order to reach Pat or one of her colleagues with whom I had made or could make contacts. In other words, I would be building a practice because I was "Mr. Pat Schroeder." This had little appeal. At best, I would be following along on Pat's skirt tails; at worst, I might be getting into an area that would prove politically embarrassing.

As the years passed, my knowledge of the workings of Congress increased, as did my friendships and many contacts on Capitol Hill. I also knew many lobbyists and lawyers who specialized in government relations practice. They were well respected, skillful in representing their clients' interests, and, as far as I know, careful to comply with applicable registration and disclosure lobbying regulations. They were, I suspect, also making a lot more money than I was.

Tommy Boggs became a good friend. Tommy was the name partner in Patton, Boggs & Blow (now Patton, Boggs LLP), one of the leading lobbying law firms in Washington. Tommy's father, Hale Boggs, was the House majority leader when he died tragically in an airplane crash in 1972. His mother, Lindy Boggs, was elected to succeed her husband in a special election in the spring of 1973 and served in Congress for many years before being named by President Clinton as ambassador to the Vatican.

Tommy built an extremely successful law firm and became a legendary Washington lobbyist and power broker. He was always careful, however, to avoid handling clients with matters directly related to his mother's committee work in Congress. I always admired and respected Tommy and marveled at the way he negotiated and mastered the political byways.

My situation and Tommy's differed. I was the husband of a young, prominent, sometimes controversial congresswoman from Denver, Colorado, home to two powerful, competitive daily newspapers and a strong opposition political party always ready and waiting. Lindy Boggs was older, a true southern lady from the one-newspaper, one-party town of New Orleans. Tommy Boggs could, like that unique city of New Orleans, march to a different drummer.

I had my road map: continue in the private practice of law, for which I had been educated and developed some experience, and which I enjoyed; earn some money; contribute to maintaining the household and raising the children; and support my political wife, but stay out of her career and avoid any political embarrassments.

When Pat looked at running for president, the *Legal Times* did an extensive look into my legal career and practice, and our family finances. The article observed that "James Schroeder will not cause his wife any political embarrassment" and that "He appears to have scrupulously avoided any appearances of impropriety." The path I took, of working in the private sector, also worked for others, such as Tony Morella.

Tony's wife, Connie Morella, was elected to Congress in 1987 from a Maryland district north of Washington that included Montgomery County. He had developed a very successful law practice in Georgetown. Tony had represented Judge John Sirica in the landmark case *Nixon v. Sirica* and was recognized as a constitutional law expert. He also taught law at American University and later became general counsel for that university.

Tony and I became great friends. As we both practiced law in Washington, we were generally available to the local media. Connie was a "local" Republican, Pat a prominent Democrat. There were few male spouses of members of Congress in those days, and of those, very few in the Washington area. So every time a local or network TV show wanted to do a story that included or focused on the views of congressional husbands, Tony and I became available targets.

We enjoyed our guest appearances as "Mr. Connie Morella" and "Mr. Pat Schroeder." I've gone back and looked at the videotapes of some of those shows, many of which were on in the morning. For some reason, I always looked too serious and tired. Tony always smiled and looked very professional. I guess I needed my pipe and lots of coffee to really relax.

Tony Morella was not only a fine lawyer and a supportive political spouse, he was also an exceptional human being. Tony and Connie helped raise nine children: three of their own and six adopted after Connie's sister died in 1972. Tony and Connie are not just role models for a successful two-career marriage but for a committed, supportive, and devoted family partnership.

I often thought that the ideal spouse for a politician would be someone in the medical profession: a doctor or nurse pursuing an independent, rewarding career and one of recognized public benefit. I saw this in Marge Roukema's husband, Dick, a psychiatrist.

He maintained a successful practice in New Jersey, was a scholarly author, and enjoyed coming down to Washington for social events but stayed out of the political limelight. Marge worked closely with Pat and was important in developing widespread bipartisan support for the Family and Medical Leave Act.

I was therefore surprised and disappointed by the public inquest of Howard Dean's wife, Dr. Judith Steinberg, in early 2004. You remember that when Howard Dean, also a medical doctor and the former governor of Vermont, began his meteoric run for the Democratic presidential nomination, a general attack against Dr. Steinberg ensued in the national press and media. She wasn't out supporting her husband on the campaign trail. She hadn't given up her medical practice to support her husband's political efforts. She had kept her own name. Obviously, this was not a healthy political marriage. Dr. Steinberg was a liability.

Now, I've never met Dr. Steinberg, but I think I'd like her, and I've admired her from afar. Apparently, the people of Vermont did too, having elected Howard governor for several successful terms.

Imagine, a community physician doing an important, rewarding, and perhaps most useful service, taking care of injured, sick, and suffering people.

To me, Dr. Steinberg is a hero who should have been admired, not attacked. She supported Howard in his political efforts in Vermont; he was elected and reelected several times. But she and Howard had a successful modern marriage, an equal partnership where each could continue to pursue an independent professional career. When Howard Dean chose to enter politics, his wife did not abandon her career. She kept her own goals; she tread her own path. Dr. Steinberg, you're my kind of people.

And then there are the Clintons, the ultimate powerful, dual-career, professional political couple. At various times each has made compromises and sacrifices. There have been significant benefits but there have also been burdens because of the other's career. Through it all, however, they have survived and succeeded.

Hillary left her promising career choices in Washington to follow Bill to Arkansas. After his first defeat for reelection as governor, she assumed her husband's name and many traditional duties as first lady, but she also maintained an independent career as a successful private attorney. Her role during the 1992 campaign and the "bimbo eruption" was critical to Bill's victory, as was her conduct during the Lewinsky affair several years later. Through it all, they raised a remarkable and charming daughter, Chelsea.

When Hillary decided to run for the US Senate in New York, Bill was her strongest supporter. During her presidential run, Bill again was with her all the way: he gave hundreds of speeches, raised critical funds, and, on balance, was a terrific asset in her historic campaign.

Contrast Bill's efforts with those of Senator Bob Doyle in 2000, when his wife, Liddy, made her own unsuccessful race, for the Republican presidential nomination. Not only did Bob Doyle (the Republican nominee for president in 1996) do very little to support Liddy, he reportedly contributed to one or more of her opponents! (Interestingly enough, Liddy was originally accepted into our Harvard Law School class of 1964 but chose not to enter. She did take a job in Langdell Library, where she met Pat, who encouraged her to accept admission. Liddy did, and graduated with the class of 1965. She even lived next door to us on Garfield Street, and one night she backed into my parked car! We're only sorry Liddy became a Republican.)

Back to Bill Clinton. According to press reports, Bill has told the Obama transition team that he "will do whatever is necessary" to avoid conflicts of interest and to position himself as an acceptable husband for Secretary of State Hillary Clinton. I am sure he will. Bill has already disclosed of the contributors to his presidential library. Bill Clinton was a very good number one. I am sure he will do his best as being a great number two.

———

From the spring of 1973, I pursued my private law practice with KKRV, and it continued for the next twenty years. In those days, the firm was unique because most of its offices and lawyers were located overseas. Its practice emphasized private and public international law matters, including litigation, arbitration, and trade and investment matters.

Maybe someday I will write more about my various cases and experiences. There were many memorable ones, and enough good stories to tell around a blazing campfire long into the night. This book, however, is not *Jim Schroeder's Legal War Stories*. But, if I may, I will tell you briefly about a few cases to give you a flavor for my experiences and practice.

For a number of years, KKRV represented the government of India in an antitrust case against five major drug companies. In a US Supreme Court decision (*Government of India v. Pfizer*), we successfully established the principle that a foreign government could sue as a plaintiff on behalf of its citizens under the US antitrust laws.

The government of South Vietnam was also a client and plaintiff in this action. When the government fell in April 1975 and Vietnam was dismissed "because the plaintiff no longer existed," I argued the issue of state succession—unsuccessfully—in the Eighth Circuit Court of Appeals in St. Paul. I knew I was in trouble when the chief justice looked down at me and said, "Mr. Schroeder, you represent this Vietcong government?" Several years later, when I told the Communist Vietnam prime minister in Hanoi that I had represented his government in its first and only action in the US courts, he laughed.

Following the release of the American Embassy employees in Iran in January 1981 and the signing of the Algiers Accords, I worked closely with my partner, Bruno Ristau, in representing and advising the government of Iran in numerous matters: government contract cases, claims by and against the US government, the tribunal cases in the Hague, and cases involving the seizure of Iranian property at the Iranian Embassy in Washington, DC.

KKRV was Washington counsel to the Embassy of Israel. I represented numerous Israeli companies in contract matters, including the company developing Israeli desalinization technology. We represented Israel in the negotiation and adoption of the Israel-US Free Trade Agreement.

Bruno Ristau and I advised the government of Pakistan regarding its purchase of F-16 fighter planes. When the US government refused to deliver the planes—which it had the right to do—we advised Pakistan that under both US law and international law, the US government was obligated to return the hundreds of millions of dollars Pakistan had paid for the planes. We were pleased when President Clinton told Prime Minister Benazir Bhutto several years later that, yes, it was wrong for the US government not to deliver the planes and to continue to keep the money.

For more than three years I worked with our Bangkok office representing the International Finance Corporation (IFC), the private investment arm of the World Bank, and the Thailand Tantalum Industries Corporation (TTIC) in connection with litigation stemming from the destruction of TTIC's plant in Phuket, Thailand. The plant was destroyed under riot conditions, and the insurance companies denied liability. The case (filed in the Thai courts) was successfully settled.

I also worked closely with our Bangkok office in representing the United Nations in arbitration proceedings involving the construction of the UN's new building in Bangkok. I prepared the arbitration claim, working with the general counsel of the UN and his deputy. (For years I enjoyed carrying around a UN identification card that identified me as an "international legal counselor.")

KKRV represented an American woman arrested in Turkey for the alleged theft of artifacts. I went to Turkey and coordinated defense efforts, including meetings with Turkish government officials. The case was sensitive because Gene LePere's maiden name was Hirshhorn. Gene's father, Joseph Hirshhorn, was a multimillionaire art collector who had established a museum on the National Mall that bears his name. The museum holds a vast collection of historic artifacts, and there was controversy about how some were acquired. Anyway, in her book, *Never Pass This Way Again*, which was also made into an NBC docudrama, Gene generously included me in her acknowledgments:

"James W. Schroeder, attorney-at-law, without whose help I might still be in Buja Prison."

As the practice of law and the shape and size of law firms evolved, so did our firm. By the 1980s, our foreign offices were larger and more profitable than our US offices. But our firm was no longer unique. Not only was Washington now full of dozens of law firms from all over the United States, but many large firms, both American and European, had established offices around the globe. For those and other reasons, our office decided in 1990 to become the Washington office of a larger, well-established New York firm, Whitman & Ransom.

I was not particularly happy with these changes, and when Bill Clinton was elected president in November of 1992, I realized that there now might be an opportunity to consider a job in the federal government, an opportunity that clearly was not available to a Democrat during the previous twelve years of the Reagan and Bush I administrations.

I had, after all, graduated from Princeton's Woodrow Wilson School of Public and International Affairs, and I believed in Wilson's legacy of "Princeton in the nation's service." I had passed my Foreign Service exams, interviewed with the CIA, and served in the US Navy. If I wanted to satisfy my long-standing desire for public service, this well might be my best, and last, opportunity.

So, after the inauguration, in February or March of 1993, I wrote letters to several friends who were joining the administration expressing my interest in a job. Well, nothing much happened.

By late spring, I talked to Pat. She said, "Look, this

is how Washington works. If you want a job, you have to identify it and go after it. You can't just say that you are generally available and wait for somebody to call you." She suggested that I sit down and talk with someone she knew on Hillary Clinton's staff to get some information, some advice, and some help.

As always, I followed Pat's advice, and as usual, it proved to be correct. Within weeks, I was offered and accepted a new job: deputy undersecretary of the US Department of Agriculture for farm and foreign agricultural services. I had forgotten that the Department of Agriculture handled more foreign trade than almost anybody and that US exports of food and agricultural commodities were one of the largest and most positive sectors of our trade balance. The Department of Agriculture (USDA) had its own foreign service, the Foreign Agriculture Service (FAS); supplied the major portion of food aid to international relief efforts; and participated in numerous multinational and regional organizations. I would be directly involved in and responsible for carrying out policies and programs in these important areas.

Throughout the entire federal government, there are only about four thousand jobs that are "political," that is, subject to political appointment, unlike jobs in the career civil, foreign, or military service systems. The highest-level positions—cabinet secretaries, ambassadorships, military chiefs of staff, and so on—are subject to US Senate confirmation. Most other positions are not. Although my position was cleared by the White House, I was appointed, technically, by the secretary of agriculture.

All of these political positions are catalogued in a book famous in Washington, the "Plum Book." I guess somebody viewed these positions as juicy, ripe for the picking, and hence "plums." In fact, many of these political plums are not filled by political appointees but by government professionals. The vast majority of ambassadors, for example, still come from the ranks of the professional Foreign Service and not through political appointments. Although positions at a number of executive agencies, such as the Office of the United States Trade Representative, will show up in the Plum Book as political, they are traditionally filled by professionals.

The reason for political jobs is the tradition in our system of government that the president should have the ability and power to bring a certain number of people into leadership positions in government, people who will administer policies and programs in a manner consistent with and responsible to that president's goals and objectives.

Certainly at the beginning of any new administration there are a lot more people seeking a political job than there are jobs available. As all the jobs are political and most will pass through the White House personnel regime, it seems safe to conclude that any successful applicant will need some political support. I'd like to think that professional competence and proven ability remain a sine qua non for any public service job. Unfortunately, politics occasionally prevails and we, as American citizens and taxpayers, are embarrassed by the appointment of a used-car dealer as ambassador to an important country or a former lobbyist for the oil and gas industry to a key position at the Department of Interior.

I was not the only congressional spouse to serve in the Clinton administration. Anne Bingaman, the wife of Senator Jeff Bingaman, was appointed by President Clinton to head up the antitrust division of the Department of Justice. Senator Tom Harkin's wife, Ruth, became president of the Overseas Private Investment Corporation (OPIC), an independent agency charged with assisting and insuring foreign investments by US companies.

Both Anne and Ruth were good friends of mine, Ruth in particular. We both accompanied Ambassador Tom Simmons on an interdepartmental trip to several of the former Soviet republics then emerging as independent states in early winter of 1994. It was an arduous, long, and a very cold trip to Belorussia, Armenia, Ukraine, and Georgia. Ruth's energy and smile added some warmth to otherwise cold, gray days filled with countless dreary meetings.

Like me, Anne and Ruth were lawyers, had had solid legal careers, and were partners in prominent Washington law firms before entering government service.

In the harsh and combative political atmosphere that surrounded the Clinton administration after the Republican Party gained control of Congress in the 1994 elections, it was inevitable that congressional spouses serving in the administration would come under some scrutiny. Anne Bingaman, Ruth Harkin, and I were among a number of spouses mentioned in an article "Democrat Power Couples" by Rebecca Borders in the September 1995 issue of *The American Spectator*, an acknowledged voice for conservative, right-wing viewpoints. Ms. Borders's attack, however, was not so much addressed to the spouses as to their congressional husbands or wives who had supposedly secured their appointments.

Pat did not "secure" my job, but the fact that she was my wife was certainly an asset. As it turned out, *The American Spectator* article was the only negative piece on my appointment that came to my attention. Perhaps major criticism by Republicans of Democratic spouses' appointments was muted by the fact that two of the most powerful Republican senators had wives who had top political jobs in the George H. W. Bush administration: Senator Phil Gramm's wife, Wendy, was chairwoman of the Commodity Futures Trading Commission and Elizabeth Dole, Senator Bob Dole's wife, was the secretary of labor.

The bottom line, then: a political spouse should not receive a government job simply because of who he or she is married to. Likewise, they should not be automatically disqualified because of their marital status. Qualifications matter. The same standard should be applied to all: education, experience, ability, and character—and certainly not just adherence to a particular social, political, or cultural agenda, as so often happened in the last Bush administration.

CHAPTER 7

# Independence

*Every marriage is a mixed marriage. In every
couple, there's one who roots thru the mixed nuts
and steals all the cashews…one who drives too fast
and one who drives too slow. The only rule for
achieving a good marriage is…to love, love realistically,
with the inoculation of experience.*
—Kathy Lette, *Altar Ego*

Within the two-career marriage, I have argued that it is not only possible but also probably a good thing for each person to continue to pursue a separate and independent career. While one career, at any given time, may have to be secondary, it still provides a source of personal satisfaction and accomplishment that cannot be gained simply by osmosis from the other partner's job. Two careers may be advisable, for economic reasons. In the case of serious illness, death, or divorce, the surviving spouse may have no choice: a job will be a necessity.

On the more personal and social side of life, I have found that some independent and separate space is also desirable, if not necessary. Many young people—especially males—fear marriage because they will have to give up their single lifestyle. Certainly there will be a need for accommodations, for compromise. But there should be room for each partner to maintain some independence. To try to do everything together may lead to unacceptable, unfair sacrifices or result in the total breakdown of the marriage.

An example: in the popular 2007 summer movie *Knocked Up*, one of the characters fears that her husband is cheating on her. He is running off to undisclosed late-night "meetings." When she and her sister follow him to a friend's house, they find out that he is not having an affair but is with his fantasy-baseball club buddies as they decide on their draft picks.

The lessons here are first, trust your spouse; second, accept that they will desire and appreciate some independent time; and third, don't feel threatened or rejected. The need to be separate part of the time does not mean that you want to be apart all of the time. Remember that old sage who told his wife: "I married you for better or for worse, but not for lunch!"

When Pat and I first moved to Denver we joined a bridge club for young married professionals sponsored by the Junior Symphony League. It was a disaster. Independent-minded, strong-willed, suspicious of authority, Pat refused to follow bidding rules. By the third or fourth hand, I was shouting, "You CAN'T bid that!" Her reply: "Why not?" A tear or two may also have surfaced. It was very clear—if Pat's eyes were not—that our marriage would not survive the bridge table. We left the party and have never played bridge together again. But we're still married!

Sports is usually the area that most guys love, whether playing or just watching. It can consume a lot of one's free time, especially when enjoyed in the company of good friends, cold beer, and warm pizza. Some women also may be bitten with the sports bug (my daughter, Jamie, comes quickly to mind), but many are not. What will marriage do to this sacred area?

In my case, I had been forewarned that my lifelong love affair with sports might need to be adjusted in the light of my new one with Pat.

On the afternoon before our wedding, we tried to play some badminton in Pat's front yard in Des Moines, Iowa. She couldn't hit the bird. She couldn't even play badminton! I was sympathetic when she explained that she had had dyslexia and an amblyopic eye. She then stepped on a bee, to which she was allergic. The next day, as she came down the aisle, she had to wear bedroom slippers because of her swollen foot. How many guys can say that their bride came down the wedding aisle in bedroom slippers?

Despite learning to fly a plane when she was sixteen, Pat was never much of an athlete or sports fan. It was one of the few flaws in her otherwise sterling character, and one that both our son, Scott, and I had to learn to live with. Pat said it was indeed ironic that for someone who was not an avid sports fan, she was the only member of Congress whose district housed four major professional sports teams: the Denver Broncos, the Colorado Avalanche, the Colorado Rockies, and the Denver Nuggets.

If I ever had good grounds for divorce based on my love of sports, it was from an incident in New York.

For a number of years, the New York congressional delegation hosted a Big Apple weekend in the city for invited members and their spouses. Pat and I joined the group on several occasions. The weekend usually included dinner at a good restaurant and tickets for theater or arts performances.

On this particular trip, Pat said she wanted to see a ballet, so on Friday night we attended a performance of the New York City Ballet at Lincoln Center.

The next morning, we joined the House Democratic Majority Leader Tip O'Neill and his wife, Millie, for breakfast in the hotel dining room. After we sat down, Tip said he was sorry about last night. Why, I asked. Tip replied, "Well, Bobby Orr was in town and I had extra tickets behind the bench for the Bruins-Rangers game. I thought you might want to join us, but Pat said you already had tickets for the ballet."

My heart stopped a beat. I could have been at Madison Square Garden watching a hockey game with the legendary Bobby Orr instead of watching some guys in tights dancing. Pat hadn't told me about this opportunity, as she knew what my choice would have been.

Grounds for divorce? You bet—at least in Canada.

I don't want to be too hard on Pat. On numerous occasions she did arrange for us to attend various sporting events, including Bronco playoff games and several Super Bowls. And she put up with her share of rainy or snowy afternoons at Princeton or Harvard or Boulder or the Air Force Academy.

The point is we all need some separate space. I really

enjoy my Sunday morning golf game with my buddies. Pat is happy at the mall, and probably more relaxed because I'm not along asking when we are going to leave. Different strokes for different folks—and I'm still trying to break a hundred.

The desire for independence, some personal time and space, often plays out in the clubs and organizations we join. Let me tell you about a venerable Washington organization, the Cogswell Society.

This group had twelve active members, and we met ten times a year. Dr. Henry D. Cogswell was a nineteenth-century San Francisco dentist and ardent temperance activist. He made a fortune during the California gold rush in real estate and mining stocks. Dr. Cogswell believed that the ills of mankind could be solved if people only drank more water, and, to this end, he donated a number of "temperance" drinking fountains to cities across the United States, including Washington, DC. Erected in 1882 at the edge of Washington's then red-light district, the fountain stood for years in front of the Apex Liquor Store, ironically enough. It still stands today at the corner of Seventh and Indiana Avenue NW, across from the Archives-Navy Memorial Metro Station.

The society was formed in 1972 with the avowed purpose of saving the fountain when its destruction was threatened by the Pennsylvania Avenue Redevelopment Commission. In practice, the society is an opportunity for its members and guests to enjoy a convivial gathering of food, drinks, ribald storytelling, and—before the new DC laws were enacted—cigars.

The membership consists of lawyers, doctors, businessmen, and government officials. Early members included cartoonist Jim Berry, TV pundit John McLaughlin, and political satirist Mark Russell. There is no prohibition of women members per se; the society holds an annual black-tie gala every January at which both sexes are welcome. But, as Pat will testify, the level of ribaldry, intoxication, and smoke leaves most women with little sense of regret that they are not full members. As Mark Russell's wife, Ali, said to Pat last year, "I wonder when these guys are going to grow up."

The Cogswell Society: a gathering of male chauvinist, sexist juveniles? Not really. A chance for a group of guys to unwind, have a few drinks, and have a good time? Probably. An opportunity to make and develop friendships with some wonderful and special individuals? Definitely.

In order to make friendships, a certain amount of time and shared experiences are required. I guess that's why we form clubs and organizations and join fraternities and sororities. When I return to my college campuses, I always stop in at my Princeton eating club, Cap and Gown, and visit the Lincoln's Inn Society at Harvard Law School. Both were the scene of many happy occasions and places where I made many lifelong friendships. We need these opportunities, and they enrich our lives. Some organizations, like the venerable Cogswell Society, provide a venue for male frivolity and independence. I'm a strong believer in the value of the "boy's night out."

Pat has her own groups as well, including an informal assembly of prominent women called "the Next Steppers,"

Gerry Ferraro, Ellen Goodman, Pat O'Brien, Letty Pogrebin, and others, who although all still working, meet and discuss their lives, futures, current events, and whatever—I'm not really sure, as husbands are not included, at least during the "formal" sessions of this informal group. We males have our own separate get-togethers, usually at a tennis court or golf course, before we all join forces for cocktails and dinner.

In the end, some independence and separateness is good. Inclusion and togetherness are better. Bert Pogrebin tells great stories, but Letty makes me think. Bob Levey, Ellen's husband, challenges my golf game and stimulates my knowledge of red wines; Ellen challenges my pen and stimulates my desire to put down some coherent thoughts on paper. I hope I've succeeded here, at least a little bit.

————

Another instance of my "separate" life was being able to pitch-hit for Pat at some event or party that she was unable to attend. As early as 1974 I traveled up to Laramie to deliver remarks to the first Wyoming Conference on Child Care. I was always a bit reluctant to speak out on substantive issues, however; political spouses often can create more distractions for their mates than provide positive support. Purely social events were less problematic, and much more fun.

Marvin Davis, an independent oil company operator, was one of Denver's and the country's wealthiest men. He and his wife annually sponsored—and Barbara continues to sponsor—the Carousel Ball, the social event of the year in Denver. Proceeds from the ball support a juvenile diabetes research center at the University of Colorado Health Sciences Center in Denver, which the Davises had endowed.

After Marvin bought 20th Century Fox studios (and Pebble Beach and the Aspen Ski Corporation), the ball took on a Hollywood flair. Dozens of celebrities and high rollers flew in from California and all over the country. The ball itself was spectacular.

On the Friday night before the ball, Marvin had a private cocktail party at his palatial suburban home for special friends and out-of-town guests. Marvin was a great fan of Pat's and a valued political and financial supporter.

One year (I've forgotten which), Congress was working overtime and Pat couldn't leave Washington on Friday. I flew to Denver that afternoon, went by our condo, and proceeded out to Marvin's in our little yellow Mustang convertible. When I arrived, the driveway was packed with limousines and high-priced foreign sedans, but I found a little spot under a big tree right across from the main entrance.

When I walked out to leave, the driveway was in gridlock, a big jam of limousines and sedans. Standing by the door, looking thoroughly frustrated as she stared at the traffic jam, was one of the most beautiful women in the world. Naturally, I introduced myself and asked if I could be of any assistance. She explained that her limo was tied up in the traffic jam and she was late for an appointment at her hotel, the Brown Palace. I pointed to my little Mustang and explained that I could get around the jam and would be happy to give her a lift back downtown. When she smiled and accepted my offer, I thought that I'd died and gone to heaven.

For the next twenty minutes, I enjoyed the pleasure of the company of Raquel Welch. Now for you younger readers, if you don't recognize the name, check out the cult movie classic *One Million Years B.C.* You won't be disappointed.

The last time I had such a good reception at the Brown was 1972, when I checked in Gloria Steinem on my credit card.

I've always admired Gloria for her wit, wisdom, and leadership. It was Gloria who observed that "Women's bodies are valued as ornaments. Men's bodies are valued as instruments." Among my treasured possessions is a pardon I received from her in 1975, "a full, free and absolute pardon for all male chauvinistic offenses against the women of the United States which he has committed, or may have committed, or taken part in, provided that such offenses are not continued or repeated." As far as I know, the pardon is still in effect!

———

There was another, more political aspect of standing in for Pat, and it also demonstrated, I hope, my desire to support her as well as carve out my own space.

Pat was, after all, an all-American girl who didn't smoke and whose drinking was limited to an occasional glass of white wine. By 10:00 PM she was ready for bed. A party girl she was not.

Yours truly, on the other hand, was "a Princeton Charley" and a US naval officer. I loved to smoke my pipe. And there was nothing better than a beer-soaked evening in the basement at Cap and Gown, unless it was happy hour at an officers' club, complete with Havana cigars.

To a degree, then, we had a mixed marriage. But then, doesn't everybody?

Perhaps I was deluding myself, but I felt that in keeping some independent space, I was still supporting, and in a sense, complementing Pat's career. If I thought I was jeopardizing Pat's success, I would certainly have adjusted my ways.

An example is a House Armed Services Committee trip to Russia in the 1980s. Long after Pat had gone to bed, I stayed up with a number of high-level Russian officials and a couple of senior male staff members of the committee discussing US-Soviet relations and arguing over various policy issues. We finished off several bottles of vodka. At one point, Georgi Arbatov, the leading US expert in the Soviet government, raised his glass and toasted me, "To Mr. Schroeder, who has followed his wife to Russia…that is, if anyone can follow Mrs. Schroeder."

Arbatov was knowledgeable about Congress and knew various members, including Pat. After that night, he also knew me. I don't know what changes, if any, were made in his briefing books, but I'd like to think that our exchanges positively affected his opinion of Pat.

Pat, after all, was operating in a man's world. She was an unknown quantity as far as committee staff were concerned, and for military liaison staff, she was a potential adversary.

Many people don't realize that the military departments have liaison offices right in the basement of the Rayburn House Office Building. I found it useful to know many of these military staff, who could be very helpful to Pat or make her life more difficult. The officers holding down these Pentagon liaison legislative offices were truly the cream of the crop, the best and the brightest. John McCain served with the navy's office after his return from Vietnam. I was quite humbled when I learned that the two pilots I was arguing with about the Vietnam War one late night in a Frankfurt, Germany, bar were both top air force aces from that war.

It is common practice in the business or legal academic world when trying to make a judgment about someone to throw his spouse into the calculation. What is this guy's wife like? What is her background? Will she fit in? What does her choice say about him?

I liked to think that my background and attitudes and experiences were pluses, and that the good relationships I established with the military had some positive effect for Pat's service and work on the Armed Services Committee.

Even after Pat retired, I continued to receive invitations to the military liaison parties on Capitol Hill.

## PART III
# Observations and Experience

*Wisdom…may be defined as the exercise of judgment acting on experience, common sense and available information…*

—Barbara Tuchman, historian and
Pulitzer Prize–winning author

CHAPTER 8

# The Smarter and More Successful the Woman, the Better

I'm so old that I still read newspapers. The third thing I need in the morning after coffee and tobacco is a paper— anywhere, anytime. I have searched hotels in Mongolia for a *Herald Tribune*, savored a *USA Today* in Belgrade, Serbia, or walked a mile in Istanbul for a *New York Times* (and some pipe tobacco—not a pack of Camels).

Of course, one should and must read the local paper. What is going on here and now, today? What are the views of local editorial writers and columnists; which national columnists are available? I'm afraid their numbers are diminishing, and the quality is disappearing.

One of the principal pleasures of a good newspaper are good columnists, people who know their stuff, have strong opinions, and can state them clearly and often with a sense of cynicism or humor. George Will, David Broder, Paul Krugman, Tom Friedman, and Ellen Goodman all come quickly to mind. They're always thought-provoking, whether you agree with them or not.

Then there's Maureen Dowd, Pulitzer Prize–winning columnist for *The New York Times*. Maureen is always worth reading. She is smart, sharp, and a brilliant writer. It's good that she is a writer. If she weren't, she would probably be wanted in half a dozen states on charges of murder and mayhem. (Thinking of Maureen makes me recall our good friend Pat Oliphant, the brilliant cartoonist, whom we first met in Denver when he was drawing for *The Denver Post*. Someone once said that it was fortunate that Pat was a cartoonist, otherwise he would be an assassin.)

Maureen is cynical and sharp as a razor blade. She can spit out venom like a cobra and cut up a public figure with the skill of a Japanese samurai. She once called Bill Clinton the Animal House president and George W. Bush the Big Emperor. Maureen wasn't very kind to my wife when she wrote a rather unflattering column about Pat's presidential exploratory efforts in the fall of 1987. Ms. Dowd's columns on Hillary Clinton during the recent presidential campaign were often abrasive and negative. One, I remember, was entitled "Clinton Jokes It Till She Makes It."

Oh well, I still love to read Maureen Dowd's columns and only wish that I could write half as well as she does.

If Maureen has a problem, though, it is that she is too cynical. She glories in taking on everybody and everything. She also tends to oversimplify and overgeneralize. Now we all generalize. I have done so in these pages. All generalizations are usually based on some facts and valid observations, but they are still only generalizations. There will always be exceptions to any rule and specific cases that cast serious doubt on the validity of a generalized observation or conclusion.

A good example is Maureen Dowd's best-selling book *Are Men Necessary?* One of Maureen's principal, if not primary, theses is that men fear and are threatened by successful women. Women, she observes, are less desirable as they become more successful. Men avoid challenging women and fear women who are smart, questioning, and use their critical faculties. Women moving up strive to marry up. Men moving up still tend to marry down.

Well, Maureen, I disagree. I think you are dead wrong.

Having taken a few shots at us men, she then lobs a grenade or two at the feminist movement of the late 1960s and 1970s. In her view, the movement was misguided and failed. Women were left marginalized and are still inferior to men. She deplores the increase in silicon and Botox injections by women who seem intent only on pleasing men, but no longer wanting to be like men.

I agree with Maureen that *Cosmopolitan* and *Glamour* are getting harder and harder to distinguish from *Maxim* and *Esquire* At one local store you can glance over at this month's *Maxim*, but *Cosmo* and *Glamour* are covered over by cardboard covers. An average copy of *Playboy* may contain an article on sexual tips. By its cover, *Cosmo* promises sexual tips, techniques, surveys, and articles each month, and every month.

The feminist movement—the movement for equal rights for women, for gender equity—was really about fairness, justice, equality, and freedom of choice. It was good for women, those who want to marry and those who didn't, as well as those who want to become professionals, work part time, or work full time at home as the much maligned but always valued housewife.

It was also good for men. I think we're all like Jack

Nicholson, looking for that woman (in his case, Helen Hunt) to whom we can say, "You make me want to be a better person." Women who make our lives more exciting, rewarding, and useful.

I always felt that feminism and romance went hand in hand, contrary to the generally accepted perception that they are in direct conflict. A recent study by two Rutgers professors concluded that feminism and romance are not incompatible and that feminism may actually improve the quality of heterosexual relationships. The researchers found that feminist women were more likely to be in a heterosexual romantic relationship than nonfeminist women and that men with feminist partners also reported both more stable relationships and greater sexual satisfaction. Who am I to disagree with the experts?

———

In the interest of full disclosure, my life has not been completely free from moments of male chauvinism. In high school and college, I dated my fair share of bimbos. There is something about the male ego. One would rather show up at the Saturday night dance with a date with a short skirt and long hair than a long skirt and short hair—and glasses.

There were the road trips, including the spring pilgrimage to Florida. My roommates and I were not looking for a high IQ from Wellesley. We were on the lookout for a 36C with a golden suntan from Florida State. When my daughter, Jamie, made a similar trip years later, she said the kiss of death was replying to some guy's inquiry, "I go to Princeton, and I'm majoring in east Asian studies and Chinese." She quickly found that by answering, "I go to Chico State, where I'm studying sociology," her social life improved dramatically.

Spring Break is one thing. The rest of the life is something else.

But even in college, the lessons were there for the learning. Yes, it was nice to walk into my eating club with that American Airlines stewardess from Chicago, but the best and most enjoyable weekends were still those I spent with the lovely and intelligent Helen Lofquist from Lawrence College (now marketing director of the Museum of Modern Art in Chicago).

The lesson here is important: the hours spent with a smart, challenging woman with a sense of humor and joy of living should be sought after and treasured when found.

One last thought: surely most men as they mature (and perhaps we do mature later than women, and then only incompletely) and seek those longer term relationships will be looking for companions or spouses or partners who are equals—or better yet, superior to themselves. There is no challenge in marrying down (whatever that means) for either a man or a woman. Life is more rewarding and more fun when you walk alongside each other. If the woman partner through ability and circumstance gets ahead, then let her lead. See where the sparks fly. When the dust settles, you will have few regrets.

I believe several of my old Princeton roommates, and longest lifetime friends, would agree.

Fred Sparling, from Barrington, Illinois, and I first met

on the American Field Service exchange student trip in the summer of 1953. His father was influential in seeing that I chose Princeton and not Dartmouth or Yale. On that trip, Fred and I met Stan Hale, from Darien, Connecticut, who also chose Princeton, and we all decided to room together freshman year. Stan was a Mormon, a direct descendent of Emma Hale, Joseph Smith's first wife.

After freshman year, we picked up additional "hall-mates," and our last two years we controlled two floors of the second entry of Foulke Hall with a group of twelve. One of the second-year additions, a fellow suitemate, was Bill Pusey, from Richmond, Virginia.

Let's take a quick look at just those three:

Fred graduated from Harvard Medical School and married his lovely wife, Joyce, while they were still in Boston. Joyce is a graduate of Wellesley and has been a college professor and medical research specialist and administrator. In her spare time she makes furniture. As for Fred, he is one of the nation's leading experts on infectious diseases, was a chaired professor and acting dean of the University of North Carolina medical school at Chapel Hill, and still teaches at both UNC and Duke.

Stan is also a doctor, a urologist in Connecticut who graduated from Columbia medical school in New York. While on an internship in Hawaii, he met and later married his wife, Sandy, a surgical nurse who was born in Canada. In later years, Sandy turned to her true love, photography. She has written a book, been in numerous exhibitions, and won many awards.

Bill married Patty soon after we graduated. Patty is a

graduate of Sweet Briar, where she later served on the board of trustees. She pursued a successful career in business and insurance. Bill graduated from the University of Virginia Law School (where else, Bill would say) and became a leading partner in Hunton & Williams, one of Virginia's most prestigious law firms (its alumni included Supreme Court Justice Lewis Powell and Senator Chuck Robb).

All three couples are still happily married. All have raised wonderful children and been blessed with grandchildren. Fred, Stan, and Bill all "married up," and I'm sure they have no regrets.

## CHAPTER 9

# What Do Women Want? Equality of Opportunity and Treatment

I recently read a review of a new book on Phyllis Schlafly, the right-wing antifeminist who led the fight against ratification of the Equal Rights Amendment (ERA) in the 1970s. My wife, Pat, was of course on the other side of this fight and remains a champion of the ERA to this day.

One evening back in the late 1970s, during the Carter administration, we went to dinner at a seafood restaurant at Washington Harbor on the Potomac River with Stu Eisenstadt and his wife. Stu was then a principal advisor to President Carter. After we were seated, the woman at the adjacent table called the waiter over and asked that she be reseated at a table at the other end of the restaurant. You guessed it: it was Phyllis Schlafly! Apparently she couldn't stand being seated near Pat Schroeder. To this day when I run into Stu, we still laugh about this incident.

The point here, though, is that while Mrs. Schlafly spent all her time and energy trying to restrict the advancement of women and to limit women to traditional and what she believed to be appropriate societal roles, Pat always fought for the expansion of women's rights and opportunities.

Probably the issue that was the most contentious and

may have proved to be the biggest impediment to passage of the ERA was the role of women in the military.

Pat had no particular desire herself to be part of the active military, but as a member of the Armed Services Committee, she worked tirelessly to see that the women who did want to serve their country and follow a military career had an equal opportunity to do so. Pat fought successfully to gain admittance of women to the service academies and to expanded roles in the services, including allowing women pilots to fly combat missions. (In 1972, women made up only 1.67 percent of the US military. By 2006, women made up 14.6 percent.)

In 2007 Kirsten Holmstedt wrote a book on American women at war in Iraq, *Band of Sisters*. In her inscription to Pat inside a copy, Captain Amy McGrath, USMC, wrote: "Ma'am, best wishes. Thank you very much for all you have done for us. Without you, we would not be able to serve the way we do now (Flying F-18's). Semper Fi."

The key here was equal opportunity: if you want to do the job and you are able to do the job, should you be prevented from doing so because of your gender or race? Who cares whether you are white, black, male, or female as long as you can do the job efficiently and effectively?

The problem seems to be that one group often tries to insulate itself and gain a sense of superiority and self-worth by discriminating against and excluding another group, usually on the basis of religion, race, or gender. So, you may say, you're a white Anglo Saxon male—an infamous WASP—what's the problem?

Well, the problem is that it is simply wrong to treat a

fellow human being as inferior simply because of religion, race, or gender. Fairness and justice demand equal treatment and equality of opportunity.

When we moved to Denver in 1964, I soon encountered instances of discrimination toward young professional women, vestiges of the past that seemed outdated, wrong, and in need of change.

My law firm's offices were in the United Bank of Denver office building at the corner of Seventeenth Street and Broadway, just across the street from the famous Brown Palace Hotel. The hotel's restaurants and bars were favorites with our firm's lawyers; the Brown's Ship Tavern remains one of my favorite watering holes. A good martini and a slab of roast beef are not to be missed here.

A good friend, Sandra Dallas, then a reporter for *Business Week* and now a noted author, having written almost a dozen books on Colorado and the West, wanted to interview me about our principal client, Vail Associates, the developer of the Vail ski area. She also said she might need a lawyer.

Weeks before, Sandra had agreed to meet a businessman at the Brown for lunch. She had arrived early and decided to have a drink at the bar of the Ship Tavern. She sat down at the bar but was refused service. She was told, politely, that the Brown Palace did not serve unescorted women at the bar. Apparently, the policy went back to World War II days, when the hotel and bar became a gathering place for single women, some of them "professionals," looking for lonely servicemen.

Sandra explained that she was a reporter for *Business Week*, that it was now the mid-1960s, and that she would like a drink, thank you very much. The bartender said no.

After I heard the story, I told Sandra I thought the Brown was way off base and I would be happy to draft a letter to the hotel's manager, which I did. I pointed out that recent civil rights acts prohibited discrimination on the basis of gender in public accommodations, as did a provision of the Colorado Constitution. As the Brown was a public accommodation, I was sure the hotel would want to change its outdated policies and serve women at its bar, thus avoiding unfavorable publicity and potential litigation.

Within a short period of time, we received a reply from the hotel manager saying that, indeed, the hotel would discontinue its old policy.

I later learned that he had called my senior partner, Jack Tweedy, who ate at the Brown every week, and asked him who the hell was this Jim Schroeder. Jack told him I was a recent Harvard Law School graduate and pretty smart, so he might want to check with his own lawyers. In truth, the Brown was happy to do the right thing and Sandra and I continue to enjoy lunch and a drink at the Ship Tavern.

Sandra Dallas was true to the legacy of those western pioneer women she often writes about. She did not want to walk ahead of men, but she didn't want to walk behind them either. What she wanted and deserved and stood up for was the right to walk *alongside* men—or in this case, sit alongside them as a measure of equality of opportunity and equal treatment.

However, if you asked Sandra if her finest achievement was being able to belly up to the bar with the guys,

I am sure she would say, "No, my finest hour was putting my belly up on a bank table and delivering my daughter!"

Sandra and her husband, Bob Atchison, had a small cabin in Breckenridge, Colorado. They had gone up for one last trip before she gave birth when suddenly, Sandra went into labor. An early snowstorm had shut down the main highway back to Denver, and there was no hospital in Breckenridge. There was a local doctor, and the best place for a delivery seemed to be a large table at a small local bank that had closed for the evening. Everything went well. Sandra later said the most annoying thing was the group of town kids who watched it all through the bank window. I guess in the pioneer tradition, necessity triumphed over modesty.

In relating this story, I can't help but recall another incident of Colorado motherhood. Diane Lazier, who had been a sorority sister of my wife's at the University of Minnesota, was living in Vail, Colorado, with her husband, Bob. From their beginning as a waitress and a ski instructor, Diane and Bob had grown up with Vail, and eventually they built condominiums and hotels there, becoming extremely successful. Bob's other love was fast cars. He later drove in the Indianapolis 500, and his two sons, Buddy—who has won that race—and Jacques, are still driving Indy cars today.

When Diane went into labor with Buddy, Bob drove her down to Denver in one of his sports cars. He was driving like crazy, and the car threw a rod on the other side of Vail pass. It happened to be hunting season. With Diane's contractions getting closer, Bob flagged down a pickup truck of hunters. Fortunately, one of the hunter's wives was a registered nurse. So they put Diane in the back of the truck, wrapped her in blankets, and headed for Denver. The only problem was that Diane had to share the truck bed with the bloody carcass of a dead deer!

All's well that ends well. As the group roared into the emergency entrance of a suburban Denver hospital, Dianne's water broke. Buddy arrived—no doubt with a sense for speed and daring that has stayed with him and served him well. I'm not sure what ever happened to the deer.

And, ladies, there are some cases where we guys are not going to insist on equality of opportunity.

———

Sometime after Sandra Dallas and I "integrated" the bar at the Brown Palace, I encountered another example of discrimination against women in the Mile High City. This one, however, was harder to deal with as it involved a private club rather than a public facility: Denver's venerable University Club.

In 1966, the Harvard Law School Association of Colorado had scheduled an annual meeting and dinner at the University Club in honor of visiting dean Ernest Griswold. Dean Griswold had a sister who lived in Denver whom we knew, and as Pat had been secretary of the Griswold Club at Harvard, it was an event we didn't want to miss. There was one other female graduate of the law school in Denver besides Pat: Zita Weinshienk. Pat and I decided to attend the dinner with Zita and her husband, Hugh, also a Harvard grad.

Well, when the four of us entered the University Club's front entrance, we were refused admission. The gentleman at the door explained that the club did not admit women, and we were thus barred from entry.

Hugh and I explained that our wives did not want to join the club; we simply wanted to attend the Harvard Law School dinner. After some discussion and assistance from several Harvard Law School friends who were members of the club, a compromise was reached: we could attend the dinner, which was on the third floor of the club, if the ladies would use the fire escape at the back of the building and enter through the third-floor emergency exit. The symbolism was perfect: the entry of women into the University Club required emergency action!

As we struggled up the dark fire escape, Pat and Zita in high heels, Hugh managed a laugh when I said, "Well, Hugh, at least they were going to let a Jewish man use the front door."

I often remember that night. Several years later Pat became Denver's—and Colorado's—first congresswoman. Zita became Colorado's first woman Federal District Court judge and served a long and distinguished career. What were those male chauvinists thinking?

Neither Hugh nor I chose to join the Denver University Club.

When Pat and I moved to Washington in 1973, I was again confronted with discriminatory club policy against women. This time it was the University Club of Washington. As the club was right down the street from my law firm's offices on Sixteenth Street and had excellent facilities, I decided to join. Plus, there was an ongoing effort by some of the members to open up the club to women. I joined that group, and after several years and votes, we were successful. The University Club became the first major club in Washington to admit women members. (The other two major downtown clubs, the Metropolitan and the Cosmos, followed suit a few years later.)

The lesson here is that change is possible and often not accomplished by outsiders but by insiders who demand that change take place. The University Club in Denver now has women members, too; perhaps if Hugh and I had joined back in 1966, change would have come sooner. I wonder what's wrong with those guys at Burning Tree Country Club or Augusta National? Would you rather play golf with John Daly or Michelle Wie?

This leads me into sports, and the Washington Touchdown Club dinner.

The dinner is a big deal. It's held each fall, honors the Redskins and other Washington sports celebrities, and presents coveted national awards to a variety of sports figures.

In 1973, Congressman Charlie Rose had two tickets that he said he couldn't use, so he gave them to Pat and me. I was excited to attend, Pat less so. (As I've mentioned, Pat was never much of an athlete. Yet though she never participated in high school or college sports, when she went to Congress she championed Title IX and constantly sought to open up opportunities for young women to fully participate in sports.)

So off we went to this black-tie spectacular at a big downtown hotel.

When we went into the pre-dinner cocktail party, I realized we were in trouble: only men were present. A hush went through the crowd as we picked up a couple drinks and decided we had better find our table fast. As we headed for the ballroom and dinner, a cordon of security officials intercepted us and said we would have to leave—right away. I quietly explained that this was Congresswoman Schroeder from Colorado and that we had tickets to the dinner, which I produced.

"You don't understand, sir," said one of the security people, "this is a stag affair. No women. No exceptions."

Pat was, of course, embarrassed, so we decided to leave. On the way out, escorted by the security people and several Touchdown Club officials, I asked one of the guys—an African American—"Well, my friend, you can't be very comfortable with this, can you?" He laughed and said, "No, I'm not, but I don't make the rules." Well, I thought, maybe you should.

Twenty years later, the Touchdown Club honored Pat with its prestigious Mr. Sam Award. Named after the legendary former Speaker of the House of Representatives, Sam Rayburn of Texas, the award acknowledged Pat's efforts in fostering and contributing to sports. The award doesn't specify *women's* sports, but that was certainly the case. The award was clearly an effort by the club to atone for its past sins. By 1993, not only were women members of the Touchdown Club, but almost half of the awardees were women athletes.

Change is possible. Change takes time. After change has occurred, we often forget the past. What was the problem?

You mean they didn't allow women to attend a national sports club dinner in Washington, DC? In 1973? Impossible!

In 1993, imagine such a dinner that did not include and honor women. Impossible! All things are possible to he—or she—who waits and works for possibilities to become realities. As the United Nations Declaration on the Elimination of Discrimination against Women states, "The full and complete development of a country, the welfare of the world and the cause of peace require the maximum participation of women as well as men in all fields." We now seem to be on the right road. The sooner we pick up the pace, the better.

CHAPTER 10

# May There Be a Generation of Children on the Children of Your Children

—Traditional Irish Toast

It's time to discuss children—and grandchildren! On Christmas Eve 2004, our daughter, Jamie, and her Aussie husband, Neil Cornish, presented us with our first grandchild, Ellie Patricia "the Sheriff" Cornish—no longer "Chiwewe," the name we had been using for the prospective heir apparent, picked off a truck stop billboard in New Mexico.

Then, on July 21, 2005, our son, Scott, and his Indian American princess wife, Amy, (Indian as in subcontinental India) had twins: William Singh and Beatrice Patricia Kaur Schroeder.

James Henry Cornish arrived on May 22, 2006, weighing in at ten pounds, three ounces. One year later he is bigger than any of the other three, and is walking and destroying everything. We call him Conan.

So, four grandchildren in less than two years. I can't help but look back to when Pat and I had our children and see some of the same lessons being repeated and learned.

First, there is no good time to have children, but some

times are better than others.

When Pat was in Congress, she gave a lot of speeches to young women on college campuses and out in the workplace. After talking about domestic and international policy issues, she would ask for questions, and invariably many of the questions would be about work and family. Almost always, some young woman would ask, "When is the best time to have children?" Pat would smile and answer, "There isn't any." For the working woman and the two-career household, there is no good time to have a baby. The experience will cause inevitable change in everybody's life and routine.

But certainly there are better times than others. Pat and I were married after our first year in law school. We both wanted to finish law school, get jobs, and settle into a new community before starting a family.

Jamie and Neil and Scott and Amy essentially followed the same pattern: complete your graduate work, get established in your profession, and then start a family—if that is what you want to do. You can't wait for a best or perfect time, because there isn't any. Though for women, the biological clock keeps ticking.

The second lesson is that the mother will have to consider and possibly readjust her lifestyle. Should she continue to work full time or work at all? Usually the husband doesn't have to face this choice.

After Scott was born, Pat gave up her full-time job as a field attorney with the NLRB in Denver and began a series of teaching positions and part-time nonprofit and community jobs. After Jamie was born, Pat worked for the State of Colorado Department of Labor as a hearing officer and then ran successfully for Congress. So a career change that arises from having children is not all bad.

When Jamie was seven months pregnant, she was hired for her dream job, as marketing director for the Museum of the Rockies in Bozeman, Montana. With some time off for each birth, she has continued her full-time work.

Amy had been on a fast track at American Express, but with the arrival of the twins, she chose to move into an independent consultant status, which allows her more flexibility and also an opportunity to pursue other clients. Her ability and talent are boundless. Whatever she wants to do and however she wishes to proceed, she will be a success.

Professor Nan Keohane, former president of Wellesley College and of Duke University and now teaching at Princeton, has observed that what we need are more on-ramps and off-ramps so women can take time off to stay at home when their children are very small, if they chose to do so, but then come back without being regarded as though their brains had rotted out. That would be better for our whole society.

Unfortunately, research using nationally representative surveys that looks at all mothers who want to return to work finds that almost a quarter can't find a suitable job and only 40 percent returned to full-time mainstream jobs (i.e., not self-employment or consulting).

Whatever parents decide to do on the job front after a child arrives, a third lesson is that you must have help. If your family can help, it is of course best, but that's more and more difficult in this day and age when families are often spread out across the country.

Pat and I were lucky: her parents, Lee and Bernie Scott, lived in Denver and were always available. We were also blessed with having some wonderful neighbors, Fern and Ed Wendoff. An older couple without any children or grandchildren in Denver, they became surrogate grandparents for Scott. They were not just babysitters; they would keep him overnight and on weekends. Ed, a contractor, built Scott an elaborate sandbox/fort and would take him on trips in his pickup truck.

Jamie missed the "Eddy-Moona" attention because she was born after we moved to Denver from Applewood, in the western suburbs. In Denver both she and Scott benefited (or coped with) a procession of live-in babysitters, au pairs, and nannies. After Pat was elected to Congress and we moved to Alexandria, Virginia, we had a succession of live-in student nannies. Katzumi, a lovely Japanese girl, was the best. Fortunately we hired her from an employment agency and paid her taxes. I remember looking in my files years later when prospective presidential appointees were becoming embroiled in what became know as "nanny gate." After Katzumi left us—she married a young employee at the Japanese Embassy—we had another student nanny, this time, a young man. When Dennis left, the kids were old enough to be left home alone—or at least they thought so. (Incidentally, Katzumi has now remarried and is living in California with her new husband and her two girls, Jamie and Christine—named, of course, after Jamie Christine Schroeder.) One of my favorite memories is coming home one night and finding the kids and Katzumi watching TV. Scott said, "We're watching

*Tora! Tora! Tora!*" Jamie looked up and added, "Yeah, and Katzumi is rooting for the Japanese."

Jamie and Neil and Scott and Amy have also relied on nannies. Jamie and Neil have been particularly fortunate, probably because they live in a college town. Ellie had her own English nanny, Heather, the wife of one of Neil's students from the United Kingdom. Later, Ellie and James Henry were under the watchful eye of Ronnie, another Montana State University student and a rancher's daughter. I can't wait for Ellie to take up barrel racing!

The point of all this is simple: if both parents are working full time, it is important and probably essential to have somebody around full time. There will be problems, and some of your help will be much better than others. And there will be others. My cousin-in-law went through more than twenty au pairs and nannies during her daughters' formative years. Nevertheless, the kids do survive and hopefully learn and profit from the experiences. As *Marie Claire* editor Lucy Kaylin points out in her book *The Perfect Stranger*, experts suggest that it's important for a child to have a strong relationship with an adult other than his or her parents. A good nanny can fulfill that role. You probably won't find a Scarlett Johansson (star of the 2007 film *The Nanny Diaries*), but you may find a Katzumi, a Heather, or a Ronnie.

By the way, I marvel at the way both Neil and Scott have grown into their roles of fathers and full partners in caring for their new offspring. Pat does too. For they are doing a much better job of supporting their wives and children than I ever did. I guess it's a sign of gender convergence.

Recent studies show that Generation X fathers spend more time with their children then baby boomer fathers did and that both sexes aspire to the same ideal, a balance between work and family. I did try to be there for our kids when Pat was tied up on the Hill, or while we were in Denver, or as we traveled around the world. On one early morning talk show, I explained to the host that when the school called me and said Jamie was sick (Pat was in a committee hearing), I left work and took her to the pediatrician. Well, when I got back to the office, there was a call from Pat: "I'll bet you $10 you don't know the name of your children's pediatrician." I laughed and said, "No, but I do know where his office is and how to get there!"

Pat was a fabulous mother. She never missed a beat: school functions, neighborhood gatherings, birthday parties, you name it, she was there whenever possible. A birthday party in the House dining room at the Capitol was a particular treat. Several congressmen still comment to me that one of their best memories of Pat is watching her stride through the Capitol with twenty or twenty-five kids in tow.

Pat's philosophy was to explain her job to the children and to include them whenever possible. Not a bad idea for any of us. So the kids knew that there were burdens that came with Mommy's job: she would be late and she would miss some school events. But there were benefits, too: there would be some special advantages and experiences.

The goal was to include the children. When Pat went to Geneva in 1973 for disarmament talks, we—the kids and I—went too, via Icelandic Airlines and using our own funds. We took the kids to Israel, the Middle East, Thailand, and the refugee camps along the Lao border. My mother believed the two most important gifts you could give your children were education and travel. We agree and believe our children do too.

But there was a problem that I never seemed to solve: cleaning up and dressing up the kids when Pat was unavailable.

The president traditionally invites the families of congressmen and high-level executive branch officials to visit the White House at Christmastime to see the decorations. For years we kept a picture of me and the kids with the Carters during one of these events: Scott is wearing corduroy pants with his knees almost poking through the worn fabric, and tennis shoes. Jamie has a dress on (not her usual football jersey), but her hair is a swirl of uncombed curls. They look like urchins from a Dickens's novel. Oh, well— at least there was no recording of Jamie asking Mrs. Carter if there were going to be nuts again in the brownies.

---

When your kids become teenagers, they start looking for summer jobs. The best place to look is often where your parents work or have some contacts. One summer Scott worked on the Capitol Hill grounds crew. He's hated gardening ever since. Jamie worked at the Capitol Botanic Gardens, but inside, on the computer.

Another "burden" of being a politician's child is just that: you are the child of a public and perhaps famous person. Jamie would often come home from school and say that a friend told her "My dad thinks your mom is stupid."

There is, I think, a double standard for children of politicians, and it does not work in their favor, as many seem to assume. I think that politicians' kids are often singled out and treated worse because of who they are. They are treated differently but not more favorably. The treatment and scrutiny that a politician's child receives is often discriminatory. Think of Gerry Ferraro's son or President Bush's daughters.

In the summer of 2007, the local papers here in Florida were full of stories regarding the arrest and conviction of Senator Bill Nelson's son on charges of battery on a law-enforcement officer. It looked to me like a case where charges would not have been brought against him except for the fact that the officer believed he had to do so *because* the individual's parent was a prominent person.

When Scott was renting a house in Georgetown his sophomore year with five other boys, the calls from neighbors complaining about "Animal House" goings-on came to me, along with threats to call the Denver newspapers. Why Scott? Why me? The pressure point was that he was a politician's kid.

It has been said that if the family is anything, it is the medium through which one generation teaches an ethical system of values to another generation. That is what the family is all about: it is concerned with the ethical rearing of children. Both Pat and I strongly subscribe to the theory that actions speak louder than words, that it is not enough to merely talk about issues and problems; one must do something about them. Furthermore, one has a responsibility to develop his or her abilities as an individual and to direct those abilities, not merely to one's own ends and satisfaction, but for the benefit of others.

Children were once the universally accepted reason for marriage. Apparently, no more. The Pew Research Center has reported that the percentage of Americans who consider children "very important" to a successful marriage has dropped sharply since 1990, and some now cite the sharing of household chores as pivotal. Children have fallen to eight out of nine on a list of factors that people associate with a successful marriage. Just 41 percent said children were very important; chore sharing was cited as very important by 62 percent. Well, then, let's take a look at household duties.

CHAPTER 11

# I Think Housework Is the Reason Most Women Go to the Office

—Heloise

The average American household operates using a fairly traditional division of labor. The man is responsible for general maintenance and heavy lifting: move the couch, change the ceiling lightbulbs, rake the leaves, clear the gutters, take out the trash cans. Cars are also a primary concern: see that the gas tank is full, the oil changed, and the tires inflated and rotated. Finally, if there are kids, and therefore toys, the husband is usually the chief engineer for toy assembly and maintenance. I can tell you that there are few experiences more terrifying than picking up a box and reading "Some assembly required."

The woman is confronted with all the rest: the cooking, the laundry, the housecleaning, the gardening, the grocery shopping, and so on.

Not only is there an obvious imbalance here, with the lion's share ending up with the lioness, but there is a time problem. Most of the "guy" jobs occur only occasionally and can be rescheduled. The trash goes out once a week, cars can be serviced on Saturday, and the gutters can be cleaned on Sunday. But as the saying goes, "A woman's work is never done." Dishes pile up in the kitchen every day. The laundry basket seems to be always full. The carpet collects dust balls and dog hairs faster than the Cubs lose baseball games.

In a two-career household, the problem is obvious. Both husband and wife return home at night after a long day at the office. Each wants to relax, to enjoy a little free time, perhaps drink a glass of wine and watch some TV or a read good book. Well, my friends, if you are sharing the benefits of those two careers—the additional family income, the job satisfaction—it is only fair that you also share the burdens, and that means that men should and must help the lioness with some of that "home work."

Frankly, I never thought much about this. Maybe it was the way I was raised. My mother loved to say, "A place for everything and everything in its place." I don't enjoy a messy house, and I like to know where things are. I'm not like Martin Burney, the husband in *Sleeping with the Enemy*, but I have been known to replace the peanut butter jar in the cabinet with the jams and try to keep the bath towels on the rack instead of the floor. Pat often observed that our house was not like Ozzie and Harriet's, but more like the Bermuda Triangle. I tried to bring some order out of the general chaos.

As for the laundry, it was largely a matter of self-preservation. For whatever reason, Pat never learned how to use a washer and dryer. The colors and whites were always tossed in together, and I ended up with pink T-shirts and dark golf-shirts covered with white lint. And they were still damp when they ended up folded on the bed!

Once I bought our son, Scott, a beautiful Ralph Lauren polo shirt. We were out somewhere, and I casually mentioned to Scott that Mom said she had done the laundry before leaving for Denver, but the clothes were still in the washer and needed to be dried. Scott was horrified: "Oh no!" he cried. We raced home, went to the basement, opened the washing machine, and sure enough, Scott's new polo shirt now looked like a rag that had been used to clean up the floor at some cheap beauty salon. Clorox and cotton polo shirts go together like warm white wine and steak: no way!

But the story has a happy ending. I bought Scott a new shirt. In later years, when he was at Georgetown, he would come back to the house and do his own laundry and also the laundry of some of his preppy roommates who didn't even know what a washing machine was. As for me, I also took charge of the laundry whenever I could. I was happy to free up Pat from this job and also save money on new shirts and towels. I never did like pink T-shirts.

The kitchen dishwasher was another issue. Pat often remarked that the trouble with men was that they thought if they turned on the dishwasher they would become sterile. Since I had a vasectomy after Jamie was born, I had no problem here. Our dog Wolfie often precleaned a lot of our dishes, so it was only prudent to round-up any dirty dishes at the end of the day and load the dishwasher, including the dishwasher detergent! Once or twice I did make a mistake and used regular soap; the kitchen floor quickly looked like a bubble bath.

I don't think anybody enjoys cleaning up the kitchen, but many women—and some men—enjoy cooking. My Australian son-in-law, Neil, loves to cook and is a marvelous chef, from shrimps on the barbi to turkey and sweet potatoes at Thanksgiving. I also understand my son, Scott, makes good spaghetti—with the assistance of Paul Newman's sauces—but I have not had the pleasure of a taste test.

I wouldn't say that I don't like to cook, but I don't love to cook. I'm okay with my grill, and I used to make apple pancakes for the kids on Saturday morning. But we've always lived just minutes from good restaurants. Why not let somebody else do the job, get your food quicker, and not have to clean up afterward?

Pat doesn't like to cook and has often made fun of her lack of culinary talent. She would joke that when she headed for the kitchen, the only one who got excited was the dog. (One evening Pat was interrupted by a phone call just as she removed a meatloaf from the oven. By the time she hung up, Wolfie, our Keeshond, had finished off the entire thing after knocking the pan off the countertop and onto the floor. I guess he was hungry!)

But Pat does make some wonderful things. Her crown rib roast is excellent and became a tradition for New Year's Eve dinner. Cherry pie is another specialty, one she initiated even before we were married. I guess she read somewhere that the way to a man's heart is through his stomach. I never really got too excited about some of her other specialties: tuna jackstraw casserole, shepherd's pie, and of course, s'mores. Believe it or not, we have a s'mores maker in our Florida kitchen today!

A favorite fund-raising project for many organizations is to compile and sponsor a cookbook. Pat would often be called and asked for a contribution. Could the congresswoman please help out with the effort and submit one of her favorite recipes? Pat's usual reply was that her "cookbook" consisted of a list of fast-food carryout restaurants, but she would try and come up with something. Perhaps her best breakfast recipe was as follows: "Find a bowl. Be sure and wash it, as the dog probably used it last. Find a box of cereal, preferably sugar coated, because you may not be able to find the sugar. Find some milk. Check the sale date. Then assemble."

Before I leave the kitchen, a word about shopping. It helps if your supermarket is open twenty-four hours a day, or at least until midnight. And it's probably a good idea if you shop together, or at least do some of the shopping yourself. Otherwise, your wife is likely to come home with all sorts of inedible things like yogurt, asparagus, salad dressing, and decaf coffee. The basic necessities are usually missing: beer, pickles, deli meats, and herring in sour cream.

The times, however, are a-changing. According to data published in *Ms. Magazine*, the average minutes spent per day on housework in the United States in 1965 was 282 minutes (almost five hours), of which men contributed only 42 minutes (about 15 percent). By 2007, the average number of minutes per day spent on housework had fallen to 214 minutes, and men were contributing 81, almost 40 percent.

———

Then, of course, there's the garden. Neither Pat nor I particularly enjoy garden and lawn work. Perhaps it goes back to our first home in Denver, out on Ward Road, in the western suburb of Applewood. We bought the house from a savings and loan association after the builder had gone bankrupt. There were no trees, shrubs, or lawn, only weeds—and I mean weeds: sunflowers and various other species, many four or five feet high. Just clearing the ground was a massive job. The trials and tribulations involved in planting a lawn and shrubs and keeping it all watered in the Denver desert while we worked all day in downtown Denver would be the subject for another book—and a tragedy, at that. Suffice it to say, whatever interest we had in gardening and lawn care died a quiet death.

When we moved to Capitol Hill in Denver, an old and established neighborhood, things were easier: maintain what you already have.

I tried to follow the same rule when we moved to Alexandria, Virginia. Our house was on a cul-de-sac, on a half-acre lot that backed up against beautiful woods and a city park area. I was happy to leave all this in a natural state. I did cut the grass and rake the leaves in the front yard, but that was about it.

Pat did her part by sprucing up the front yard and filling up our window boxes and flowerpots with plastic and silk flowers bought from a local Thai importer. The red geraniums were particularly pretty—until they turned pink after several months of rain and sun. Some of our neighbors were a bit embarrassed, but not as much as Pat's aunt from Nebraska. A doctor's wife and former nominee in a Mrs. America contest, she was at first shocked by her niece's lack of gardening skills. She then laughed and complimented Pat on her ingenuity and resourcefulness.

Pat was really caught one day when a gardening magazine called and said they were doing a story on the gardens of members of Congress and wanted to feature hers. Pat replied she was sorry, but she didn't have a garden. The editor said, "No, everybody says that, but everybody has a garden."

So a week later, a camera crew arrived. As they were unpacking the editor drove up, walked around the house, looked at the lawn—and silk flowers—and told the crew to pack up. He looked at Pat and said, "Well, you were right. You don't have a garden."

————

If the way to a man's heart is through his stomach, they way to a woman's is with flowers.

It took me a while to get the message. Once I sent Pat a dozen roses on her birthday. When I got back to my office after a breakfast meeting, several secretaries looked up and started laughing. When I asked what was so funny, they handed me one of those telephone message slips with a message from my wife. It read: "Some roses came with your name on them. It must be a mistake."

Needless to say, I tried not to forget any birthdays after that, although one year I had a close call.

I was working in my firm's Bangkok office when I picked up the morning English-language newspaper, the *Bangkok*

*Post.* I just happened to glance at that little box: famous people born today. Included on the list was Congresswoman Pat Schroeder. Oh my God, I thought, I'm in trouble. But then I remembered that if it's July 30 in Thailand, it's still July 29 in Washington, DC. I quickly sent off a telex to my secretary (yes, those were the days of telexes and faxes, before the Internet and e-mails) asking her to send Pat birthday flowers. She did—probably with a smile, remembering that phone memo—and I was saved again.

I've always learned from Pat. Say thank you. Give a compliment. Send flowers. The best way to feel good is to make somebody else feel better. As St. Francis of Assisi said, it is in giving that we receive.

CHAPTER 12

# Women as Friends and Colleagues

*Women are not an object.*

—Graffiti on the back of the Coyote Ugly bar behind
my apartment in Washington, DC

Several years ago, the Sunday morning NBC news had a segment that caught my attention: Can men and women simply be friends? The commentator noted that as more and more women enter the workplace and in light of the recent sad events coming out of the military, the question has become one of significant interest. Of course, they had to begin with that classic film clip from *When Harry Met Sally*. You remember the scene: Billy Crystal and Meg Ryan are driving back to New York from Chicago. Billy says it can't happen; the sex thing always gets in the way. Meg says no and protests that she has a lot of male friends—just friends. Billy smirks as only he can and says smugly, "You only think so!" Billy may have been right about Meg Ryan. But I believe he is wrong as a general proposition. And that was the thrust of the program segment. NBC had a man and a woman on who worked together. They claimed that they could work together and be good friends—and that's all. There was also a psychologist on who had written a book or at least studied the issue. He outlined his rules for maintaining such a successful relationship. I didn't have a pen and paper handy, and I don't recall all of his key rules, but the bottom line seemed pretty obvious: use common sense and know what you are doing.

I was struck, however, that he didn't emphasize what I feel is the key: treat your fellow worker with respect and as an equal—at least in regard to the personal relationship aspects of the situation. Naturally, relationships are complicated by authority: who works for whom, who is the boss; by age: who is older and more experienced, who is younger and perhaps less secure; and by circumstance or status: who is married or single, which person is a member of a perceived superior social class.

When everything is said and done, any relationship between a man and a woman should be based on mutual respect and equality. That, to me, is the answer. As a man, I do not approach a woman as a lesser person to be dominated or used, and certainly not as an object to be possessed or conquered. A woman should be equally independent and responsible. She can and should have as much control over any situation as the man. She has the right to expect and to be able to maintain a respectful and equal relationship. She also has some responsibility, especially if she is bright and attractive, to approach the relationship with a firm sense of where things may go, depending on what choices are made. I'm still old-fashioned enough to believe that the signals sent out by the female are critical and that most guys will respond accordingly.

Let me give you an example. I worked for several years on a fascinating legal case in Thailand. (I'd love to tell you more about this, but that might be another book.) One of the lawyers I worked with was a young woman associate of a major London city firm. Catherine was younger than me, very bright, and very attractive. A classic English face, high cheekbones, wispy blond hair—a shorter version of Lady Di. And she was married, as of course was I. Slightly different circumstances: I'd been married for over twenty years and had two great teenagers; Catherine had just been married three years, with no kids.

We worked together off and on in Thailand for relatively long periods of time over the space of three years. We came to be great friends. We enjoyed each other's company. We had many great evenings together in Bangkok, a city drenched in Oriental sensuality. We visited bars, went out with friends on late night escapades, hit the discos, often stayed in the same hotels. We maintained a "professional-plus" relationship of friendship based on respect and trust. We regarded each other as equals, and together we figured out how we could keep and manage our relationship, one which we not only enjoyed but valued.

Later, Catherine became one of the first woman partners in her firm due to her outstanding ability and talent. I hope that my recommendation to her partners was some help. And she is now a proud mother of two fine children.

———

One of the unfortunate facts of life seems to be that as we grow older, we have fewer and fewer opportunities to make and sustain good friendships with members of the opposite gender. Let me tell you about one such experience I was lucky enough to have.

For a number of years, I was privileged to be the token male member of the congressional wives' book club.

The "godmother" of the club was Jeanne Simon, and rightly so. Her husband, Paul—first congressman and then senator from Illinois—was a gifted writer in his own right, having written over a dozen books before his death. Other founding members included congressional wives Elinor Bedell (Berkley Bedell), Elisabeth "Debra" Leach (Jim Leach), Gayle Kildee (Dale Kildee), and Nina Solarz (Steve Solarz). The group also included a number of Senate spouses: Ann Simpson, Barbara Levin, Shirley Metzenbaum, and Ernestine Bradley.

We tried to meet every month or so, and each time one member would be responsible for selecting the book (although this was often done by consensus) and hosting the venue, including dinner. This led to some difficulty in my case. When my turn came, Pat was tied up on the Hill with congressional work. Faced with the prospect of serving dinner to eight to ten congressional wives, I naturally took the coward's way out and sent my daughter, Jamie, over to Peking Gourmet for Chinese carry-out. The food was excellent, but Pat was appalled when she came home and saw that I hadn't even dumped the food from the cardboard containers into nice serving bowls.

I did do better, however, on my book, selecting Rick

Atkinson's *The Long Gray Line*, the story of the West Point class of 1966. I chose it because one of the prominent figures in the book was Dr. Jim Ford, dean of the West Point chapel. A good friend, a very special person, Jim was at the time chaplain of the US House of Representatives. I invited him to attend our meeting. He, of course, knew many of the book club members—or their husbands—and it was a wonderful experience for all of us to talk with Jim as he shared his experiences from those tumultuous days.

This was a special feature of our book group. Because, I suppose, of our membership, we often were able to include either a special person associated with our book selection or even the author. I remember Nina Solarz selected *Life and Death in Shanghai*, written by a Chinese woman, Nien Cheng. Her book detailed her six years of solitary confinement at the hands of the Red Guards. She was able to join us. It was truly a memorable evening.

The book club was also especially good for me, for I was forced—I would now say privileged—to read many books that I would not have chosen on my own. We were not an early version of Oprah's book club, but we did read a number of books that opened new horizons for yours truly. I tend to be heavy on history and politics, balanced by fiction, usually on the mystery and adventure side. One evening at Barbara Levin's, Carl suggested I try Elmore Leonard, and I have been grateful ever since.

The value of the book club was threefold. First, it provided an opportunity to share views and discuss issues of importance: history, poetry, religion, culture, family, personal relationships. When I was in the navy, the rule was that in the wardroom, you were not to discuss politics, religion, or women (it might have been sex, but in the navy the two are synonymous). Most social conversation tends to follow the same rule. With the exception, of course, of politics in Washington, DC, we just don't talk about serious subjects. The book club offered this opportunity.

Second, as I mentioned earlier, we all had the chance to expand our horizons and read new and different things, and thus think about and talk about new areas of interest and concern. The great thing about college was continually being exposed to new ideas and fields of interest. As we move on through life's journey, we often become stratified, our views narrow, our opinions set. The book club was a vehicle to continue to grow and to learn.

Finally, for me our monthly gatherings provided an opportunity to make a number of lasting friendships with wonderful women. I often think that one of the downsides of having a good marriage in our current culture is the subsequent failure or inability to make and sustain good friendships with the opposite sex. I'm very glad that since law school, through my years of law practice, politics, and government service, I have met, worked with, and made good friends with a number of remarkable and talented women. As a result, my life has been made much richer, enjoyable, and certainly better.

So, you guys, join a book group—especially if it's full of smart, interesting women. As Grigg learned in the 2007 summer's film, *The Jane Austin Book Club*, you may find you have been missing out on some marvelous reads—as well as wonderful friends.

# PART IV

# Some Additional Thoughts from a Politician's Husband

CHAPTER 13

# Political Sensitivity

When asked about political marriages, I answer that in my experience, the most successful ones are those in which the nonpolitician spouse possesses political sensitivity. When you have someone in the political public eye, I think the other party has to understand what that entails.

It also helps to enjoy politics and the political world. I knew several spouses of members of Congress who did not enjoy politics, and they were the ones who tended to be unhappy.

For me, there was no question that I enjoyed politics. As I have written earlier, I wrote my senior thesis on Adlai Stevenson's governorship in Illinois while I was majoring in politics, history, and economics at Princeton's Woodrow Wilson School of Public and International Affairs. After we moved to Denver, I was active in local political campaigns and party organizations and ran, unsuccessfully, for a seat in the Colorado House of Representatives in 1970. Finally, I played a major role in Pat's campaign and election to Congress in 1972. Through my background and experience, I developed a love for politics and some good political instincts, which served both of us well.

Elsewhere in these pages, I have also discussed my

own career choices and some of the political considerations I weighed in that process.

Political sensitivity had a bearing on a number of
other choices we made. Pat and I were strong supporters
of the public schools, both being products of the public
school system. We both signed the complaint in Denver's
landmark school desegregation case, *Keyes v. School District
No. 1.* But in 1973, the public schools in the District of
Columbia were already in trouble, and even our most liberal friends, such as Don and Arvonne Fraser (Don was the
Democratic congressman from Minneapolis), advised us to
live in the suburbs. So we ended up in northern Virginia,
where Scott could attend a public grade school in Fairfax
County. We enrolled Jamie in Head Start, which she loved,
and for which we paid tuition. Where you live, how you
live, where your kids go to school are all personal decisions, but decisions that can have political consequences.

Nevertheless, one of Pat's later Republican opponents
did attack her for living "in a lavish Virginia mansion"—a
politically motivated overstatement if I ever heard one.
Since most of the Denver local press had visited our modest 1950s-era tract home, which I purchased literally over
the phone in December 1972, the story quickly died.

One's financial affairs can be a problem area. After Pat
was elected, I reviewed our stock portfolios and sold any
holdings that I thought might present a political conflict of
interest or embarrassment, such as stock in defense-related
companies or natural resource industries. (Similarly, in the
summer of 2007 the Clintons decided to sell millions of
dollars worth of stocks out of concern that their financial

affairs could become a political liability for Hillary.) I also decided to prepare our tax returns so that I personally could explain any deduction or answer any potential question about our personal finances. This was, by the way, even before later congressional financial reporting requirements were enacted. I filled out those forms, too. In addition, Pat released summary information from our tax forms each year, although this was never required.

As an aside, even this Harvard lawyer had to quit doing our tax returns after Congress passed the Tax Reform Act of 1986, meant to simplify the tax code. Simplify? What a joke! It should have been called the "Bureaucratic Obfuscation and Accountants Welfare Act." But that's another story, and as Dennis Miller would say, "Now, I don't want to get off on a rant here..."

Some congresswomen who turned over their financial affairs to their husbands got into big trouble. The classic case was Enid Greene Waldholtz, a Republican from Utah. Young, attractive, and smart, the GOP quickly targeted her as an up-and-coming potential star. Her stay in Congress was very short, however, and her marriage ended in divorce. Soon after being elected, her husband, Joseph, briefly disappeared. He was later charged with illegally mishandling his wife's campaign funds and embezzling family money.

Eleanor Holmes Norton, a Democrat elected as the District of Columbia's delegate to Congress, did somewhat better and remains in Congress to this day.

After she was elected, I got a call from the Democratic Spouses Organization. They followed a practice of assigning one of their members to the wife of each newly elected congressman. That member would offer to assist the wife in getting settled into Washington and the congressional scene. Since there were so few husbands of congresswomen, I was asked to offer advice and assistance to Mr. Norton. I was happy to do so.

When I called Ed Norton, a Washington lawyer, he was cold and curt, even unfriendly. He wanted no advice. He said that he didn't want his wife to run; it was her idea, and as far as he was concerned, she was on her own.

It turns out that Mr. Norton may have been anticipating the future scrutiny that would inevitably come with Eleanor's election. The press soon discovered that the Nortons had failed to file any tax returns for several years. Eleanor claimed that she had trusted her husband and didn't know he had not filed their returns. Her political career survived, but the Norton marriage did not.

I suppose the best-known case illustrating the embarrassment and potential damage that a husband's financial and business affairs can cause his wife's political fortunes is, unfortunately, that of Geraldine Ferraro and John Zaccaro.

We first met Gerry and John after Gerry was elected to the House of Representatives. They have remained good and close friends ever since.

I remember, however, our first night out together in Washington. We had a nice dinner and talked extensively about Gerry's successful campaign and the current political scene in Congress and in Washington generally.

I found Gerry smart, full of energy and ability, and attractive to boot. I guess that's why I've always liked Gerry: she's so much like Pat.

I also liked John: warm, friendly, and also very smart. He had a New Yorker's confidence enriched with a good Italian American sense of family loyalty and pride. He was the kind of guy you immediately wanted to have as a friend, and I have been enriched by his friendship.

As we drove home that night, I did tell Pat that I was surprised and somewhat concerned by John's apparent lack of political sensitivity. He seemed to possess excellent business acumen and solid street smarts, but I worried about his political antenna. He had discussed Gerry's campaign financing and his New York business and real estate interests. He seemed too confident that his life would remain unaffected by Gerry's election.

Gerry's selection by Walter Mondale as the Democratic Party's candidate for vice president in 1984 was a great day and a step forward for the Democratic Party in particular, and for both women and the country in general. For John Zaccaro, however, the early rainbows quickly disappeared only to be replaced by the dark clouds of persistent and often unfair media investigation and criticism.

I don't begin to know all the facts or even remember the various details. I do remember that Gerry did an unbelievable job explaining and defending their tax returns at a four-hour press conference. There was a lot of bad publicity about some of the New York real estate holdings, but John eventually survived, probably a wiser—and certainly a poorer—businessman and political spouse for it.

From the time we were married, Pat and I held most of our assets in joint tenancy. After moving to Washington, I met a young woman investment advisor with Shearson

Lehman Brothers. P. J. Hovey (she hated her real name, Paula, which I rather liked) was smart and sensitive to my investment concerns. I said that because of Pat's position as a congresswoman, a member of the House Armed Services Committee, and a public figure faced with disclosing our holdings each year, I wanted to avoid any defense-related investments or stocks that might prove embarrassing. If that meant a more modest portfolio performance, so be it. She understood. We bought Procter & Gamble instead of GE.

P. J., by the way, is another remarkable career woman. She relocated to Georgia and still handles our accounts out of the Smith Barney office in LaGrange (wherever that is). Ah, the wonders of modern-day communications. At least she is in the United States—although we Floridians do have doubts about Georgia, especially during football season.

———

To sum up, then: in a successful two-career marriage—and, I suppose, in the case of a one-career family as well—it is preferable if not essential that the spouse understand, appreciate, and even enjoy the other partner's job or profession: the pressures, the demands on time, the constraints, the detriments as well as the benefits. In the political arena, the most supportive spouse is probably one with good political sensitivities and one who enjoys politics.

Let me give you several examples, fellow husbands of congresswomen who enjoyed supporting their successful political wives. There were very few of us around in the early 1970s, but these were some of the best.

I got to know most of these fellows during a two-week Congressional Delegation (CODEL) trip to China during the end of December 1975 and early January 1976.

President Nixon and Secretary of State Henry Kissinger made their historic visit to China in early 1972, when Nixon became the first American president to visit the People's Republic of China (PRC). By the time Gerald Ford became president, in August of 1974, only one congressional delegation had visited the PRC, consisting of senior leaders in the House—all men. In 1975, Margaret Heckler, then the senior woman in Congress, with the support of Chinese government officials argued that the second delegation should be women, and President Ford agreed.

As I now recall, the delegation consisted of ten—a majority—of the seventeen women then serving in Congress. Five of the seven married congresswomen were joined by their husbands, including me.

It was a memorable and historic trip. The delegation was the first to have a long face-to-face meeting with Deng Ziaoping, who was emerging as the leading "moderate" power in the PRC. (This was still the era of Mao Zedong's supreme leadership and the Cultural Revolution. Deng was purged by the Gang of Four in April 1976, then rehabilitated after Mao's death. By 1977, he became the acknowledged power in the PRC.)

Our delegation also was the only group of high-level US officials in Beijing when Premier Zhou Enlai suddenly died in early January 1976.

The meeting with Deng Ziaping, which took place in a fancy reception room somewhere within the Great Hall of the People, was, to use a good southern vernacular term, a hoot. Deng was quite short and was swallowed up by his big Chinese stuffed chair. He chain-smoked Panda cigarettes, enveloping himself in a cloud of pungent and thick gray smoke. He was friendly, but seemed ill at ease in the company of a bunch of women, particularly US congresswomen.

The format for the meeting was that after some opening pleasantries and introductory remarks from Deng, each congresswoman, in order of seniority, would be allowed to ask one question. When Bella Abzug's turn came, she asked a rather long question, the thrust of which came down to "What is China's policy toward Israel?"

After Deng's interpreter finished whispering in his ear, Deng frowned, looked at Bella, and then turned and shot out a wad of spit into the large old-fashioned spittoon next to his chair. Deng then smirked and mumbled something to his interpreter, who looked over at the congresswoman seated next to Bella and said, "Next question." Bella was dumbstruck. I almost laughed.

As our group was walking out of the Great Hall, I noticed that Martin Abzug, Bella's husband, had fallen behind the rest of us. In fact, he had stopped walking and was surrounded by a dozen or so of our Chinese escorts with whom he appeared to be engaged in a spirited, animated conversation. I speculated that Martin might be trying to smooth over Bella's concerns about Israel with our hosts. So I went back and asked Martin if he was having a problem explaining Bella's question. Martin laughed and said no; he was just trying to explain to the Chinese how the Dow Jones Average worked.

On another occasion, Martin emerged from a rather primitive Chinese men's room with everybody laughing, both Chinese and Americans. "What's going on now, Martin?" I asked. "Oh," he replied, "the Chinese are very curious, so I was explaining circumcision to them."

That was typical Martin Abzug. A successful Wall Street stockbroker, he didn't particularly like it when Bella ran for public office, but he supported her 100 percent when she did and always with a sense of warmth and humor. He complemented Bella, who was known for her flamboyance, tenacity, and independence. When the National Women's Political Caucus established their "Good Guy Award," they named it in honor of Martin Abzug.

I certainly didn't attend all the meetings with our Chinese hosts. Chinese bureaucrats can be long-winded, and the necessary translations resulted in lengthy meetings. Not being an active participant, I looked for alternative activity.

I had been told by a newspaper correspondent who had been on the earlier Nixon-Kissinger trip that good Havana cigars were readily available in Beijing and they were cheap. Martin Abzug had expressed his desire for a box or two, so I decided one morning it was time to go shopping.

I was joined by Bill Burke, who was also bored with Chinese lectures. We snuck away from our Chinese handlers and headed for Beijing's main shopping street, which was just around the corner from our hotel.

Bill Burke was married to Yvonne Brathwaite Burke, who had been elected to Congress from a Southern California district in November 1972, the same time as

Pat. A small, stunningly beautiful young African American woman, Yvonne collected "firsts." She was the first black woman in the California state legislature, the first woman to chair the Congressional Black Caucus, and the first congresswoman to give birth to a child while in Congress.

Bill was a handsome, no-nonsense businessman who had grown up in Zanesville, Ohio, and had sparkling blue eyes that would rank right up there with Paul Newman's.

As we walked down the crowded streets, we created quite a stir. Remember, this was December 1975. There were virtually no foreigners in China at this time. Among the masses of gray-, black-, and dark-blue-clad Chinese, we stood out like sore thumbs: an African American, with blue eyes no less, in a fashionable overcoat and a Caucasian wearing a Stetson and smoking a pipe. And, of course, we both towered over the crowd by at least six inches.

We were soon being followed by dozens of curious onlookers. When we stopped to shake hands with some beautiful little Chinese kids, the mothers didn't know whether to smile at or run in fear from these foreign devils.

Our objective was the Beijing Department Store, the largest store in town. Once inside, I tried on a beautiful Chinese silk dressing gown. Burke took one look and said, "That looks great; it should sure help Pat with the gay vote in Denver." I decided not to buy the gown.

As we were leaving, we could not help but notice a very attractive blond Western woman looking at purses at one of the counters. She was wearing an attractive jacket, stylish boots, and a wool skirt. (When we returned to the United States, I told friends that during two weeks in

China, the only Chinese women I saw in dresses were on the stage at the Beijing opera house.)

Bill walked up and introduced us: "Hi, I'm Bill Burke, from Los Angeles. This is Jim Schroeder, from Denver. We're here with our wives, who are attending meetings with Chinese officials. What do you do?" She smiled and said, "I'm the wife of the Canadian ambassador." Without missing a beat, Bill replied, "Well, would you like to go somewhere and have a drink?" Laughing, she answered, "My, you really are from LA!"

Another day, the Chinese arranged three different field trips for the congresswomen. The first would visit several neighborhood schools and focus on the Chinese educational system. The second would stop at a hospital and acupuncture clinic, with an opportunity to examine the status of healthcare in China and the interrelationship of Western and traditional Chinese medicine. Finally, a third trip was scheduled for a visit to one of China's largest turbine factories.

Each member was given a choice of which trip to join. As you might suspect, all of the women chose either the educational or medical facilities option. None of the ladies expressed an interest in visiting a turbine factory, especially when they learned that getting to the plant required an hour and a half bus ride from Beijing.

When the Chinese realized that no one had signed up for the factory tour, there were obvious signs of concern, and even fear, among the hosts. I guessed that if none of the foreign delegation showed up at the factory, there would be plenty of "lost face" to go around, both for the government officials who had arranged the visit and for the factory managers and workers standing by at the plant.

I went over to the Chinese and explained that the women, being wives and mothers, were understandably more interested in medicine, healthcare, and children's education, but I, and perhaps some of the other husbands, would be delighted to go on the turbine factory tour.

The Chinese seemed to understand and were obviously relieved and pleased that they would not have to cancel the factory visit.

I was able to corral one other spouse to join me, Reuben Spellman, the husband of Congresswoman Gladys Noon Spellman. Gladys was elected to Congress from a suburban Maryland district just over the eastern borders of the District of Columbia in the post-Watergate Democratic landslide election of 1974. Her congressional career ended, tragically, in the fall of 1980, when she was running for her fourth term. Gladys suffered a heart attack and then lingered on for years in a coma. She finally died in 1988. In recognition of her many years of public service to the people of Maryland, and also, I think, of her years of sickness, the Baltimore-Washington Parkway was renamed the Gladys Noon Spellman Parkway in her honor.

Reuben was actually excited to visit a Chinese turbine factory. He was a professional engineer with Westinghouse, which was then in the business of building power plants.

When we finally arrived at the Chinese factory, I knew we were right to have made the effort. We were met by several dozen plant, government, and Communist Party officials—and the plant's local band! An elaborate

Chinese reception had been set up: dumplings, tea, and plenty of mai tais for all kinds of toasts to Chinese-American friendship.

What I found incredible, though, is that most of the ten thousand to twelve thousand workers at the plant had been turned out to greet us and to cheer or clap at the appropriate time, as signaled by the plant's general manager. With banners flying and the band playing, Reuben and I thought we were at a military change-of-command ceremony at Fort Meade or Fort Carson.

The actual tour of the plant was interesting. Reuben asked intelligent questions, often expressed satisfaction with the products, but shook his head in disbelief at the working conditions and practices we saw.

We were glad we went. It was a day well spent. We hoped we had been of some assistance to our wives and complemented their work. We weren't along just for the ride. We hoped we had made a positive contribution to a successful congressional trip.

After a long, gray, cold Chinese day, it was always a pleasure to return to the hotel and enjoy a glass of good scotch and conversation with Bob Meyner, the husband of another member of the delegation, Helen Stevenson Meyner.

Robert B. Meyner was a distinguished ex-governor of New Jersey, having served the state from 1954 to 1962, which covered the four years when I was at Princeton. Bob had the foresight to bring along his flask and a bottle of scotch. Again, remember, this was December 1975. To the best of my knowledge, there were only two Western-style bars in all of the PRC: one in the old French concession hotel where Nixon stayed in Shanghai, the other in the Peking Hotel in Beijing. We stayed in both, and I enjoyed telling people that I had had a drink in the only two bars in China.

Unfortunately, the choices at those bars were either Chinese beer or Great Wall wine. Even when warm, the Chinese beer was drinkable; the Great Wall chardonnay was not.

Bob Meyner was the classic example of a powerful man who accepted a new subordinate role to his now more politically active wife. He had no problem stepping out of the spotlight and assuming a secondary but nonetheless fully supportive place at their partnership table.

In sum, then, I traveled with four different congressional spouses: Martin Abzug, a warmhearted, successful Jewish stockbroker from New York; Bill Burke, a talented African American businessman from Los Angeles; Reuben Spellman, a professional engineer from Maryland; and Bob Meyner, the patrician ex-governor of New Jersey.

They all shared some important things in common. They loved their wives and supported their wives' political careers with sensitivity and enthusiasm, even if from a secondary of subordinate position, and they loved their own lives, which included independent careers and the opportunity to stay involved in politics and public policy, which they tried to do with good judgment and a sense of humor.

Why not marry up?

Why not let women walk alongside men, or even lead?

These men, I think, would say it makes for a sometimes challenging but always interesting and rewarding life.

———

Let me add here a few thoughts about congressional travel.

During her twenty-four years in Congress, Pat traveled a great deal and was often criticized in the press for doing so. As far as the press was concerned—or at least some self-appointed media watchdogs—congressional delegation trips, or CODELS, were simply junkets, vacations for members of Congress at the taxpayers' expense. As far as they were concerned, nobody really worked, and the fact that members were often accompanied by their wives or husbands proved the point.

Well, as one of those husbands who was lucky enough to join his wife on many CODELS, I couldn't disagree more. Every trip I took, I believe, was justifiable, valuable, and well worth the cost. I'm not sure the total for all such trips in a given year would even register as a small blip in the Pentagon's annual multibillion dollar budget. And they were hardly vacations. All you had to do was look at the schedule of a typical trip and know that if your own travel agent booked such a "vacation," you would never go.

In particular, I always thought it was extremely important for members of the Armed Forces Committee to visit our bases and troops overseas, to see firsthand their living and fighting conditions. Did they have adequate facilities, enough of the right equipment? Did our military leaders and commanders appreciate the concerns of our country's elected representatives?

Moreover, any military man will tell you there is no substitute for experiencing the geography of a place. Sure, you can look at a map, but it's not the same as flying in a helicopter up the valley following the main road to the DMZ and realizing that Seoul and its 10 million souls are only thirty miles from the North Korean border. It's much easier to understand the tensions and issues in the Middle East after standing on the Golan Heights in former Syrian gun emplacements, looking down on the Israeli farms below.

Should members of the House Judiciary Committee have visited the refugee camps in Thailand in the 1970s after the fall of South Vietnam or the Afghan refugee camps in Pakistan during the Soviet Invasion of Afghanistan in the 1980s as they considered immigration legislation? I believe so.

The experiences of foreign travel and its lasting effects on individual members and eventual influence on policies or legislation could be dramatic. In Pat's case, she would always meet with our Foreign Service officers. As a result, and as chairwoman of the Civil Service Subcommittee she became a cosponsor and champion with Chairman Dante Fascell of the House Foreign Affairs Committee of major legislation in the 1980s to reform the US Foreign Service.

As chairwoman of the Armed Services Subcommittee on Military Construction, Pat was able to increase the jurisdiction of that subcommittee to include "burden sharing," getting our allies (particularly in NATO) to bear a fairer share of defense spending. Her efforts, ably assisted by her Republican colleague David Martin, led to several important trips, perhaps the most successful one to Japan. A series of meetings with the highest leaders in Japan's government and diet, or parliament, helped consummate

Japan's contribution of more than $6 billion to the costs of the Gulf War.

Lest there be any doubt about the importance of foreign travel and the power of an individual congressman to affect US policy, one need only turn to the case of Charlie Wilson. Charlie's role in supporting and arming the Afghan mujahideen in their war against Russian invaders has been vividly told in George Crile's book *Charlie Wilson's War*. The movie, starring Tom Hanks and Julia Roberts, was terrific.

CODELS often provided our ambassadors and agency (CIA) personnel with access to top foreign government officials and to information that they could not obtain on their own. Many a US ambassador's first face-to-face meeting with a foreign head of state came when hosting a CODEL'S visit.

CODELS were also an important factor in helping to establish and maintain the atmosphere of bipartisanship and mutual respect that prevailed in Congress throughout the 1970s and 1980s. When you travel with people and perhaps also with their spouses, for a week or ten days, you get to know them, their backgrounds, their congressional districts, their concerns, and their areas of expertise or interest. That's a good thing. Pat learned why her colleague from South Carolina would have trouble supporting a bill expanding employment rights for women—and that Pat might have trouble getting elected from Columbia, South Carolina.

The rise of partnership and increased lack of mutual respect and accommodation on Capitol Hill in the 1990s coincided with a falloff in congressional travel. With fewer and fewer opportunities to build friendships, it becomes easier to make enemies.

CHAPTER 14

# The Media

*Good night, and good luck.*
—Edward R. Murrow

Politicians and the media coexist in a hazardous world. Politicians seek and often crave publicity. Reporters are constantly in search of news: stories that will sell newspapers and place their byline on the front pages. As the saying goes, if something isn't in the press or on TV, it didn't happen. On the other hand, sometimes an incident or event is reported that didn't happen—or at least didn't happen in the way it was publicized.

Often articles covering the same event are dramatically different. On several occasions, I would marvel at the reports in *Time* and *Newsweek* of an event at which I had actually been present. If you read the articles, you would conclude that the reporters had been attending a different event.

Headlines can also be deceptive. Written by editors and not the reporter who wrote the article, they can express a conclusion or point of view that the article itself does not fairly support.

For a congressional spouse, the press was a reality,

a presence always to be reckoned with. Sort of like my daughter's pet cat, Mao: fed regularly and petted often, she was a pleasant addition to the family, but if ignored or mistreated, she could create havoc.

Jane Sanders is married to Bernie Sanders, the former congressman and current senator from Vermont. Reflecting the feelings of many congressional spouses, she once observed that the hardest part of being in politics or of being married to a politician was waking up with a knot in your stomach as you wonder what is on the front pages of the newspaper. You know it may not bear any resemblance to the truth, she said, but you still have to deal with it.

Every political spouse has probably developed his or her own rules for dealing with the press. Dennis Thatcher, husband of former British prime minister Margaret Thatcher, had this advice: "Ignore the press, and simply do not respond to their questions or request for interviews."

I elected to follow a different path. I had always been an avid newspaper reader and a devoted follower of the TV news and talk shows. Many reporters and columnists were friends, or at least good acquaintances. I admired their craft and respected their professional responsibilities. If they wanted to talk to me, I would be happy to talk to them.

There remained one overriding concern: not to embarrass my politician wife or become a problem or separate source of controversy.

Dan Buck worked for Pat throughout her congressional career. Beginning with the 1972 campaign, Dan provided Pat with loyal support, tireless effort, trustworthy advice, and astute political judgment. He also had a great sense of humor.

Dan realized that Pat's family, and particularly me, could either have a positive or a negative influence on Pat's political career. As a standard to follow with respect to my own personal and professional conduct as well as relations with the press and media, we came up with the "Al Gordon Rule."

Al Gordon was a young reporter in the Washington bureau of the *Rocky Mountain News*. He was smart, aggressive, and somewhat combative. He took any press release with a certain grain of salt. Al didn't have much experience covering Washington, and I don't think he had much use for politicians, but he was honest and tried to be fair and balanced in his reporting.

So the Al Gordon rule went like this: before undertaking some professional obligation or personal activity—really, in a sense, before doing anything—be prepared for a call from Al Gordon. Be able to talk and answer questions about the event in an honest and forthright manner. If you cannot explain or defend you actions, don't do it. If you can but only with difficulty and complicated explanations, you're better off avoiding those situations too.

It was a good rule, a precautionary principle. Always try to think ahead. Where the potential harm is great, the prudent course is to exercise an extra degree of caution and restraint. Trouble can't always be avoided, but it's usually worth trying.

Pat and I both enjoyed and benefited from good relations with the press and media. Because she is smart, articulate, attractive, and blessed with a sharp wit and sense of humor, Pat was sought after for her views and opinions on myriad issues and became a regular on the TV news programs and talk shows. To a far lesser degree, but with similar positive treatment, I received my share of press and media coverage.

I guess it began with Pat's first winning election. On November 22, 1972, Dick Tucker, a political writer for the *Rocky Mountain News*, wrote a column titled "Friendly look at Mr. Jim Schroeder." Dick had decided it would be fun to "profile" me along the lines of previous articles about politicians' wives. Dick was an old friend and a skilled political reporter, and I was happy to cooperate.

Dick wrote that "Perky Jim Schroeder, sometimes known as Mr. Pat Schroeder...tactfully dressed in a dark sports coat and slacks...The vivacious brunette voiced some apprehension about the upcoming social scene in Washington." Anyway, you get the picture.

Dick and I thought the column was a hoot, and most readers did, too. There were, however, and surprisingly so, quite a few complaints by men objecting to what they saw as my demeaning and degrading treatment as a woman. Funny, isn't it, when we treat a man the same way we do a woman, it can reveal more about perceived gender differences than the treatment itself.

Being a loyal spouse and a good lawyer, I had to resist writing letters to the editor every time I read an article or editorial that criticized Pat. Certainly any such reporter or editorial writer had his facts wrong or did not understand the issue. In the earlier years of Pat's congressional tenure,

I did write a few such letters. I still have a copy of a letter I wrote Bill Hornby, the editor of *The Denver Post*, in May 1980 when *The Post*'s editorial board had written something questioning Pat's leadership abilities. A wiser course, however, was to leave this type of political skirmishing to Pat's capable staff—Sally Brown, Kip Cheroutes, and Dan Buck—all of whose quivers where filled with barbed arrows sharper and stronger than mine.

―――――

Probably Pat's most unpleasant tussle with the press occurred during the Carter administration: "Bunny Gate."

Several years after the congresswomen's trip to China, a delegation from the House Armed Services Committee was invited overseas in order to meet with Chinese political and military leaders as well as visit a number of Chinese military bases. Pat and I were part of this CODEL.

The trip was scheduled during the congressional Easter recess, as were many such CODELS. Having been in gray, gloomy Beijing before, Pat wanted to do something special for the US Embassy Foreign Service kids. She knew the CODEL was invited to the ambassador's Easter party and egg hunt. The week before, in Washington, she had rented a big fluffy bunny suit and papier-mâché head, which she wore at an event escorting Colorado's Cherry Blossom Festival princess (it was, incidentally, a big hit). As she still had the suit, she decided to take it with her and wear it to the embassy egg hunt.

To the delight of Ambassador Leonard Woodcock and

Deputy Chief of Mission Stapleton "Stape" Roy, Pat—the Easter Bunny—was the star of the party and egg hunt. All of the kids and their parents were thrilled by this touch from home.

As Easter Sunday was a free day, most of the CODEL went on a bus tour out to the Great Wall after the party was over. Pat left the suit and the bunny head in a bag on the bus. After returning from our hike on the wall and awaiting the return of others, Pat got the bunny head out and started showing it through the window to passing Chinese families. (The rabbit is some kind of good luck symbol in China.) Soon, a crowd full of smiling Chinese kids gathered in the parking lot. So Pat got off the bus, briefly put on the bunny head, waving to the kids, and then let some of the kids hold the head. It was all great fun and lasted about five minutes.

Well, when the CODEL arrived in Japan on the way home, the phones were ringing. Apparently some wire-service stringer had filed a story based on second- and thirdhand accounts that Congresswoman Schroeder had spent Easter on the Great Wall in a bunny suit handing out candy eggs to the Chinese people. You can imagine the uproar, and it wasn't even clear what kind of a bunny suit she was wearing.

By the time the CODEL got back to Washington, the initial firestorm had all but died down. The wire service, after doing some checking, apologized and retracted its story.

Buzz Larson, *The Denver Post's* chief Washington political writer, interviewed Pat, who confirmed that she had not worn a bunny suit and handed out candy to the Chinese on the Great Wall. *The Post* also wrote a retraction story.

One of Pat's detractors on the committee—perhaps a fellow member or Republican staffer—then sensed an opportunity for political mischief and called Larson, telling him that, in fact, Pat *had* worn a bunny suit at the Great Wall and mingled with a group of Chinese.

Buzz was furious. He thought that Pat had not been truthful with him, and he didn't want to let this matter go away.

I knew Buzz well and considered him a good friend. He was, however, from the old school. He wasn't excited by the new, younger, and more liberal Democrats who were being elected in Colorado (Tim Wirth, Gary Hart, Dick Lamm), and he certainly had doubts about a young liberal woman. He once told me at a cocktail party, "You know, the problem with your wife is that she thinks she has to pick up every sparrow with a broken wing."

I tried to explain to Buzz exactly what had occurred concerning this matter. After all, I was there. In the end, Bunny Gate blew over with no real harm done, and the world moved on. The only loser in all of this, if there was one, was Buzz Larson, who remained bitter for years to come.

In his or her dealings with the press, all a politician can ever hope to do is to be open, honest, and genuine—and then let the chips fall where they may. I wouldn't have taken a bunny suit halfway around the world and worn it at an Easter egg hunt in China, and I know Buzz Larson wouldn't have either. But Pat Schroeder did, and a lot of Foreign Service officers and their children enjoyed a very special Easter because of her thoughtfulness and generosity. Pat is different and unique and special. Very special. I guess that's why *The Denver Post*, Buzz Larson's old paper, named her one of the ten most memorable Coloradans of the twentieth century.

————

To be open and honest with the press and media may be difficult, but that is still not enough to ensure fair treatment. Anyone who has been in public service or in the private business or legal world, for that matter, has probably experienced at least one instance where he or she encountered a stacked deck. You know when you are being questioned by a reporter with a specific preconceived agenda. The interviewer is seeking something to support the opinion or conclusion that has already been made.

To mislead or be untruthful with the press is a dangerous gamble. To try to evade or challenge legitimate press inquiry is asking for trouble, though what is legitimate may be subject to debate. The sad case of Senator Gary Hart, Donna Rice, and the good ship *Monkey Business* comes quickly to mind.

I used to believe that the worst thing a member of Congress could be, as far as the press was concerned, was a phony. Somehow, like sharks in the water, the press can sense the presence of blood, and then strike out at its victim. But I now realize that it is not the press that brings down a politician; it's the people. The press, after all, does not make the news; it reports the news. It may pick and choose which events to cover, and in that sense "make" the news, but the press does not plan or make the event itself.

Two examples: Congressmen Gerry Studds and Barney Frank. Both were close friends of ours, as were their partners. Gerry served in Congress for many years before retiring, and he compiled a distinguished record for his constituents. Barney continues to serve, now as the chairman of the House Financial Services Committee. He is, without doubt, one of the brightest minds and sharpest wits in the House. Both Gerry and Barney are gay. They came out of the closet in part because of press scrutiny. Each suffered some unfavorable publicity, Gerry's involving a House page, Barney's concerning an alleged paid companion. Nevertheless, both admitted they were gay, apologized for certain questionable behavior, and were reelected by their constituents. They were not phonies.

In contrast, we have the case of Bob Bauman, a Republican congressman from the Eastern Shore of Maryland. Staunchly conservative, Bauman was in the forefront of preserving Christian values and attacking any suggestion of gay rights. Thus, when it was reported that the congressman had been having affairs with young men, his constituents reacted by voting him out of office. Bauman was a phony. Senator Larry Craig suffered a similar fate.

———

Thomas Jefferson is reported to have said that if he had to choose between a democratically elected form of government and a free press, that he would choose a free press. But, it's not enough to have a free press. We need an independent, aggressive, curious, and professional press and media. We had it in the Vietnam era of the 1960s and 1970s. We did not have it during the run-up to the Iraq war.

But there are signs of life returning to the Fourth Estate. There are new sources of information and discussion, some of which this old dinosaur doesn't even understand: What's a blog? Where is My Space? (I thought it was here!)

Anyway, my friends, keep reading, stay informed, and keep your fingers crossed!

CHAPTER 15

# "Yes, Dear": The Dennis Thatcher Society

*At last—a club for men whose wives wear the pants.*
—*National Enquirer*, October 10, 1995

In life in general, and in politics in particular, it is good to have a sense of the ridiculous and to keep a sense of humor.

Back in the early 1980s, I was browsing through *Washingtonian* magazine one evening when an article caught my eye regarding the formation of a new, somewhat mysterious organization: the Dennis Thatcher Society. The columnist observed that in a city traditionally dominated by powerful men, there was now a refuge for the husbands of powerful women.

The godfather of this society was Charles Horner, then a midlevel bureaucrat with the United States Information Agency but more importantly, the husband of Constance Horner, then head of the US Office of Personnel Management (and later deputy secretary of the Department of Health and Human Services). Horner explained that he felt it was time to have a club for the husbands of women who were both powerful and the subject of media attention while the husbands themselves remained obscure.

Moreover, Horner observed, he was continually intrigued by the many comments and questions he received from friends regarding his own status: What was it like to be eclipsed by your wife? Are you not threatened by your wife's success? You must be jealous. How do you control your anger? How, in a word, do you survive?

Reflecting on his status and such questions, Horner noted that his situation in life was not entirely dissimilar to that of the husband of then British prime minister Margaret Thatcher. Hence the name for the organization: the Dennis Thatcher Society.

But why Dennis Thatcher? There were, after all, other husbands of prominent women who might be a suitable namesake. Horner explained that Dennis Thatcher was indeed the perfect role model for his new society: a man who clearly was not threatened by his more powerful and prominent wife, a woman whom he loved and supported. With a good sense of humor (and a glass of scotch), Dennis Thatcher was content to remain out of the limelight as much as possible.

What really got my attention, however, were Horner's comments about the society's membership. He explained that of course the society was still in its formative stage, But when pressed about its membership, either at present or in the future, Horner stated that Jim Woolsey "was probably" a member. At that time, Jim Woolsey, a former under secretary of the navy, had returned to private law practice in Washington. His wife, Suzanne, a successful economist, was a high-ranking official at the Office of Management and Budget. (In 1992, President Bill Clinton appointed

Woolsey as his first director of the CIA.) Certain men who were members, Horner explained, knew they were members—"like Jim Schroeder, Pat Schroeder's husband."

Within the next day or two, I couldn't resist calling Mr. Horner. I was anxious to learn more about an organization to which I knew I belonged but about which I knew nothing.

I had never met Charles Horner, but I was immediately impressed by his obvious intelligence, sharp wit, and terrific sense of humor. He said he had received numerous calls about the Dennis Thatcher Society since the piece had run in the *Washingtonian,* but he explained that he couldn't tell me much about the society because "there really wasn't much there yet." He said he did appreciate my call and that as a fellow-founding member, the only appropriate thing to do was to get together, perhaps with several others, for an initial meeting of the society.

Before we could ever get together I too began receiving media calls about the society. News of the society's formation had apparently spread like wildfire, with press items appearing not only in US papers, but also in papers around the globe. Horner and I began to play phone tag. One day I'd call Charles: "Charles, I just got a call from Melbourne, Australia. I told them what I could, but I then told them to call you." The next day, Charles would call me: "I received a call from the *Guardian.* They wanted to talk to some other members, so I told them to call you."

The media interest in the society was always a source of fascination and amusement to me, and to Charles. Initially, of course, the heavy degree of interest we received from the British Commonwealth was attributed to the fact that we were, after all, the Dennis Thatcher Society. Given the traditional place of private and exclusive clubs in the United Kingdom and its former colonies, it should be expected that newspapers in Ireland, Australia, or Canada might be interested in learning more about the purpose and membership of a club formed in Washington, DC by some husbands of prominent American women politicians who had chosen Dennis Thatcher as their role model.

The British Commonwealth private club rationale did not explain, however, the interest from South America and Asia. I was interviewed in depth at least twice by reporters from major Japanese newspapers. And in both cases, they were younger women reporters. One kept calling me back every year or two wanting to keep up on the ongoing activities of the society. I began to see a pattern. People were not simply intrigued with some new old-boys club; what they were interested in was the idea that some men who were married to politically powerful women were able to not only "allow" their wives the prominent role, they could accept that fact and assume a secondary and supportive position. Moreover, these men were apparently not jealous of or threatened by their wives' success and were able to take it all with a sense of humor.

We did finally manage to convene the first formal meeting of this very informal society at the Cosmos Club in Washington. This first meeting—and I use the term advisedly—set the tone for the society's future mode of operations. First, it was not at all clear who in fact was a member or if they were informed of this first luncheon gathering. Horner called a few people whom he thought should be members, including Tom Harvey, a prominent Washington lawyer whose wife, Cathleen Black, was the publisher of *USA Today,* and I called one or two others. Second, we thought it entirely appropriate that we meet at a club where one of our wives was a member and where we could sign her name for the bill. In this case, Horner's wife, Constance, was the member of this old and prestigious club, and indeed one of the first woman members after the club finally gave up its all-male status sometime around 1980.

At this first meeting, attended by Horner, Woolsey, Harvey, and myself, we reached consensus on the principles for the society's future existence. In addition to the goal of meeting only at a club where we could sign one of our wives' names, these principles—which, of course were not to be formally adopted or written down—were as follows:

- The society vowed not to elect officers or maintain any membership role.
- There would be no written bylaws, rules, or records.
- We did agree on adoption of a slogan, as most private organizations or fraternities have some special utterance or handshake that captures the essence of the organization and binds its members together. The slogan of the Dennis Thatcher Society would be "Yes, dear."

Well, that's how we began, and I suppose we still exist, although I haven't talked to Horner for some time. Over the years, we did have a number of good times. There was a memorable dinner with our patron saint himself. Actually, it was a dinner for Dennis sponsored by British Conservative Party supporters in Washington to which we were invited as special guests. Of course Horner and I went, and we were delighted to sit at Dennis's table. He was interested in our society and its purposes, which we explained. We found Dennis a thoroughly charming fellow with a good sense of humor and a keen appreciation of how his words and actions could either help or hurt his wife Margaret's political career.

Several years later our ranks were increased by the addition of Steve Lowey, a New York antitrust lawyer and husband of New York congresswoman Nita Lowey. I'm not sure how, but Steve came into possession of a letter written in 1992 from Dennis Thatcher to one James Hoskinson, whose wife had been elected president of a riding club in Connecticut. Hoskinson asked for advice and suggestions from Thatcher, saying his "need for a role model as the first husband of a club president" was obvious.

Dennis's reply was a classic. After stating that he wasn't sure about the similarities between the spouse of the president of a riding club and the spouse of the prime minister of the United Kingdom, he nevertheless offered the following guidelines for spousal conduct. They reflect Dennis's wit, and wisdom, and I quote them as follows:

• Never ever talk to the press, local or national. A smiling "good morning" will suffice. Remember that it is better to keep your mouth shut and be thought a fool than open it and remove all doubt. Avoid telling them to "sod off"; it makes them cross.

- Never ever appear speaking on TV. This is the short road to disaster.

- Avoid being photographed holding a drink in one hand and cigar or cigarette in the other. This brings cosmic obloquy from the teetotal and anti-smoking lobbies, and they *will* write voluminously to you and about you.

- Never make speeches longer than four minutes, and prepare them very carefully to ensure that there is no possible quote. This results in the press not ever reporting you were there at all.

- When visiting or opening factories, i.e., horseshoe manufacturers, saddle makers, animal feeds, etc., take the elementary precaution of reading their last annual report so you know what sort of corporation it is and whether it makes any money, then you can ask moderately intelligent or tactful questions.

- When members of the club approach you with complaints and suggestions as to the conduct thereof, listen attentively and then say, "I will pass on your excellent comments," and then forget it.

- Avoid the small function whenever possible. The annual picnic for the stable boys on Lincoln's birthday can be deadly. Carry a flask so you can lace the Coca-Cola, but don't get caught doing it.

- Avoid any possible run-in with the police or FBI as this tends to attract unfavorable comment.

- After the first seven years there is risk of overconfidence. Guard against this, for there is a mantrap for the unwary every day.

- The price of keeping moderately trouble free is everlasting vigilance and the strict observance of the above rules of the game.

- To be serious, the job is easy. It is love and loyalty, as simple as that, plus a bit of common sense.

As for the media rules, I am sure these probably were meant with tongue in cheek. But one of the things that always amazed Charles Horner and me was the media interest in our "organization." One of the early pieces was a full-page treatment in *People* magazine. The piece was memorable, for we did it at the British Embassy in Washington. The staff at the embassy got as much of a kick out of this special meeting of the Dennis Thatcher Society, complete with life-sized cut-outs of Dennis and Margaret, as we did.

Another phenomenon was that each article seemed to trigger more and new interest in us. In the fall of 1995, an article in the *National Enquirer* set off a new wave of calls that Horner and I had fun passing back and forth. Many calls simply wanted more information on who belonged to this organization and when and where we met. I explained to a reporter that sudden success by a member could disqualify him from membership in the society, as happened with Dick Cheney. Dick's wife, Lynne, was head of the National Endowment for the Humanities. When Dick Cheney was simply a Republican congressman we considered him a member. As Horner observed, "There's nothing more obscure than a House Republican." Then Dick Cheney became secretary of defense and simply too prominent to remain eligible for the society.

Not every superwoman's husband was eligible for membership. The element of obscurity was crucial. As Horner once observed, "Bob Dole couldn't possibly be a member." Bill Clinton would be unable to join the society on the same grounds. One of our more memorable meetings was hosted by Director Woolsey in his private dining room at CIA headquarters in Langley, Virginia, in 1993. The occasion for that luncheon—beyond, of course, enjoying the special privilege of seeing Jim in his official digs and touring the agency's museum—was to officially welcome Professor Martin Ginsberg of Georgetown University into the society. Although a well-known professor of tax law at Georgetown, Ginsberg had not qualified for membership in our society until his wife, Ruth Bader Ginsberg, eclipsed him by ascending to the US Supreme Court. Our other justice spouse, John O'Connor, Justice Sandra Day O'Connor's husband, was unable at last moment to attend and welcome his new colleague.

In 1997 I received a call from an editor at *Esquire* magazine. He asked about the society, and we had a lengthy chat. It was clear that his interest as someone married to a prominent businesswoman was how two-career marriages survived, especially where the woman becomes the more successful and prominent of the two. I guess the best advice I could give was to quote Dennis: "The job is easy. It is love and loyalty, as simple as that, plus a bit of common sense."

On the evening ABC news one night, Charlie Gibson did a piece on the oldest living married couple. A British couple, whose name I didn't get, had been married eighty years. The husband was 103 or 105 and sat there, half awake, occasionally nodding off. The wife, also about 100, was more chipper and did all the talking.

Naturally, the subject of the interview was love: the nature of true love and how the couple had stayed married for eighty years. As the old gentleman seemed to fade in and out, the woman talked on and on, explaining that it hadn't always been easy those past eighty years and it had taken some compromises, at which point she turned and nudged her husband. His eyes blinked wide open, his head became more erect, and he turned and said, "Yes, dear."

It seems we members of the Dennis Thatcher Society knew what we were about when we selected our motto.

# Conclusion

So, dear reader, we come to the end of our journey together. I hope you have not been disappointed. In fact, I hope that you have received some value for your time and money. I hope you enjoyed and will perhaps benefit from my experiences, wisdom, and humor—my tales as an old congressional spouse.

I have written about my own background and about my exceptional wife, Pat Schroeder. About heredity and environment. About chance and choice.

Where two careers are involved, it is best to avoid competition and be prepared to compromise. One spouse may have to accept the realities of second place while supporting the other's career as best as he can. You can, however, maintain a separate career and independent space.

Women are special, and the smarter and more successful, the better. Women want equality of opportunity and of treatment. They deserve no less. Men will benefit, as will society in general. Children are special and worth the effort, and their care should be shared, as well as household work should. Additionally, you can have women as friends and colleagues and they will enrich your life.

There are special considerations for the political spouse, but they can be faced with a sense of humor and due regard for the press.

By now, readers will have figured out that I am a movie buff. I love movies, and one of the best parts of retirement is having more free time to catch a new film at my local theater or an old film on TV or DVD.

In the summer of 2007, I particularly enjoyed *Freedom Writers* starring Hilary Swank. Hilary plays Erin Gruwell, a high school teacher in a tough inner city school who helps transform the lives of her students when she has them write letters to Miep Gies, the woman who helped Anne Frank's family hide from the Nazis. Somehow, Erin's professional husband fails to support her; he wants to control her, to monopolize her—so of course, he loses her. That's lesson one: support and cooperation rather than strife rooted in envy produce success. When your wife succeeds, you will prosper and benefit, as well as will others, in this case, the schoolkids.

But there is a second lesson here, too: treat others—your wife, your children, your neighbors, your fellow man or woman—as you want to be treated yourself. Yes, the good old Golden Rule.

Thinking of Anne Frank reminds me of a lecture I heard one afternoon at a Princeton reunion by a young woman professor who had studied the stories of various Dutch families during the German occupation in World

War II. She had tried to answer this question: When Jewish neighbors or friends came to the door seeking help, shelter, or refuge from the Nazi authorities, why did some of their fellow Dutch citizens say yes and open their doors and hearts, and why did others say no, closing their doors and thus a last hope for safety?

The results of her study appeared clear: there was no thread she could identify that helped explain the individual decisions. Neither religion, education, social status, nor economic standing gave an explanation. Indeed, there were cases when members of the same family— perhaps a brother and sister—living in the same community and with all the same identifying factors came to opposite decisions: one opened the door and offered assistance, the other did not.

Life is a series of choices, and the quality of our lives, our marriages, our families, and our society depends on the choices that we make.

David Halberstam, the great writer who died in 2007, wrote that every nonfiction book should be written to answer a question. My questions have been these: How does the dual-career couple survive? How do you live with a talented, smart, challenging woman? I've tried to relate through my experiences some answers. You walk down life's highway together and if necessary, let her lead. You share the burdens as well as the benefits. You treat your wife, your children, your colleagues, and your neighbors as you want to be treated. It's love, loyalty, and a bit of common sense. I trust I made some good choices, and I wish you, dear reader, good luck as you make yours.